# Need and the National Health Service

## ECONOMICS AND SOCIAL CHOICE

A. J. Culyer

UNIVERSITY OF YORK

Martin Robertson

First published in 1976 by Martin Robertson & Co. Ltd.
17 Quick Street, London N1 8HL


ISBN 0 85520 091 X (paperback)
ISBN 0 85520 092 8 (case edition)

Typeset by Santype (Coldtype Division) Ltd., Salisbury.
Reproduced, printed by photolithography and bound in Britain at The Pitman Press, Bath.

# Need and the
# National Health Service

ECONOMICS AND SOCIAL CHOICE

*York Studies in Economics*

GENERAL EDITORS: Professors Alan T. Peacock and Jack Wiseman

ECONOMIC POLICIES AND SOCIAL GOALS
*edited by A. J. Culyer*

THE VALUE OF LIFE
*M. Jones-Lee*

WELFARE ECONOMICS: A LIBERAL RESTATEMENT
*Charles K. Rowley and Alan T. Peacock*

# Contents

# Preface

This book has been written for all those who are concerned with, or about, the NHS. In so aiming for a readership that comprises many experts in various specialisms relevant to the health territory, as well as the layman, I may have attempted the impossible. If so, I can scarcely hope to have succeeded. Since, however, the question of the need for health care is not a question for any single set of experts – or necessarily one for experts at all – it seems to me important to try to communicate with as wide a set of people as possible. I believe that even economists may find something of interest herein, for though I have done my best to drop all jargon (though I doubt if I have entirely succeeded), my colleagues in economics will be able readily to see 'elasticities of substitution', 'utility measurement up to a linear transform', 'compensating variations in income' etc. lurking behind some of the verbiage that replaces it.

Thus, while the perspective is that of the economist, I have both avoided (so far as I can) his jargon and have avoided specifically identifying what the economic perspective *is* (as compared with what it is *not*). Together these amount to a crafty attempt to demonstrate that the perspective is no more than a systematic and commonsensical way of thinking about the problem of choice – in this case, the problem of collective or social choice. The reason for this is that the solutions to the problems we confront can be found only by multi-disciplinary research and fact-finding. Economics, while being far too important a subject to be left to the economists, is at the same time tarred in the eyes of some with the brush of commercialism and free markets, an impression I am anxious here to avoid, so that the important differences between disciplines (which are their strengths) can be brought to bear on the common set of problems rather than on the trivial apparent differences that divide them. Economics, as the science of choice, can lay bare the necessary elements in making social choices about meeting needs for health care, and its techniques can also provide empirical estimates of the dimensions of some of the relevant elements. But many elements are also clinical, epidemiological, aetiological, sociological, administrative, etc. Economics provides, I believe, the integrative element — but although a necessary element, it is by no means the *only* necessary element. Since the days of the polymath are long past, I can only hope that my colleagues in other disciplines will not judge my forays into their territory too harshly — even when I have been a little critical. I have also been compelled to be somewhat critical of economists; so, if I have been intemperate on occasion, I trust I have been even-handed about it and always, at the very least, courteous.

This book is not really new. The core ideas have all appeared in print elsewhere (often more than once!), the principal ones being an article in *Social Trends* on health indicators, written jointly with Alan Williams and Bob Lavers, and a short *pièce d'occasion* in *New Society*. In addition I have not hesitated to pinch the good ideas (published or unpublished) of many friends and colleagues — though I hope I have admitted such thefts sufficiently for the true owner to be identifiable. Finally, the research programme in health economics at the University of York has its own ambience and 'oral tradition', which is a kind of collective property upon which I have also freely drawn. I believe, however, that there is value in trying to set out between the covers of a single book a way of thinking about health policy that has much to offer all those who care about the NHS — and even those who don't. The book should be seen as complementary to similar themes advanced by others, in particular the extremely readable epidemiological book by Professor Cochrane, and Professor Cooper's equally readable economics text, both of which — to prove I acknowledge my intellectual debts — are frequently referred to in what follows. I have attempted both to provide an integrating context for the study and solution of a set of problems that are recognised by nearly all those who work in the health territory, whatever their disciplinary allegiance, and to go further than has been gone before in developing a way of resolving these issues.

Economists will be surprised at my conversion to the language of 'need'. At one time, indeed, I had quite convinced myself that the word was an incubus on the back of any serious student of the NHS or of health problems in general. I am now however equally convinced that, accepting the definition given it in this book, it is an indispensible and profoundly useful tool of both analysis and policy. While economists were at one time regarded with extreme suspicion by the traditional students of the NHS because of mistaken beliefs about the desirability of political attachments rather than analytical straight thinking (only good socialists made good students of the NHS) and an equally mistaken belief about their commitment to things pecuniary, such general suspicion is now well on the wane – as it indeed should be. A new suspicion, however, is almost bound to arise from the line of thought put forward here, and this will probably derive from a no less mistaken belief that economists (or this one at least) trust in the perfectability of social controls or, less strongly, in the invariable beneficence of social controls. Moreover, since not all the ideas to be developed here have as yet been fully worked out or tested, there will be ample ammunition for those whose first response to a new idea is always 'it's impossible', 'we know best' or 'how are you going to make it work?' rather than 'how can we improve on it further?' or 'how can we make it work?'

Such are the ramifications of a proper notion of 'need' that each thread of the logic cannot possibly be traced through within the compass of a book such as this. But it is, of course, this very quality that makes the agenda for research into need and health so exciting – the core ideas and the ways in which they can be applied are becoming clear, but so much work remains to be done. It is particularly encouraging that much of this work is being undertaken in Europe, especially that with the support of the DHSS (in England) and OECD (in Paris).

What this book represents, then, is an attempt to set out some core ideas that relate to one another both directly and indirectly through the concept of 'need' to form what Imre Lakatos (according to Mark Blaug) has called a 'scientific research programme'. I have attempted to do this in simple language and without the clutter of jargon so that non-economists can see – and evaluate – what is going on. And I have also tried to show explicitly how, why and where pure science – in both the 'classification' sense and the 'testable hypothesis' sense – must be impregnated with ethical judgements. Since this book is not a blueprint for the reform of the NHS, empirical and administrative material and problems have been introduced only for illustrative purposes. Those expecting a blow-by-blow account of the economics or the organisation of the NHS had better look elsewhere.

It would be unconvincing to deny, however, that, though the book is not a blueprint, it is also not intended as a prolegomenon to reform. Indeed, the driving ideology behind it is precisely that a truly humanitarian, fair and efficient NHS can be evolved *only* if we travel along the path indicated here, and so I have emphasised the issues and the concepts, the ends and the means, rather than playing the administrative games that so often pass for analysis in the health field and of which the recent massive reorganisation of its administration was a magnificent example. But the substantiation of this grand claim will be very much up to others in the 'programme' — wherever their location and whatever their professional affiliation — to substantiate.

Finally, a brief word about the bibliographies after each chapter and the 'Questions' section at the very end. The bibliographies, while far from exhaustive especially in the non-economic areas, contain more than is referred to in the text. For those wondering where to go next in their reading and who are unfamiliar with the literature, references in the text provide the easiest way of identifying other people's work that is seen (at least by me) as being closely linked with what has gone on in the chapter. Beyond this, the titles of articles and books should be sufficient to indicate content.

The 'Questions' section was added at the last minute at the suggestion of Alan Maynard on the grounds that the sort of question often discussed in my seminars with students may prove of use to other teachers in the health territory. They may even amuse the ordinary reader. While it was not my intention to write a 'textbook' on which a course in health economics could be based and which may be used by students in preparation for exams, I suppose there is the possibility that it may be so used. However, while the questions could serve the purpose of providing topics for some seminars relating to themes in this book, they by no means cover the full range of material discussed. Their chief purpose is to provoke students into a speculative and critical frame of mind, in which they can both detect bunk and not be able to evade the real issues; it is not to test their understanding of the substantive 'message' (such as it is) of this book.

# Acknowledgements

My first and foremost debt is to my colleagues at York in the DHSS-financed programme of research in health economics and the SSRC-financed public sector studies programme. Although the projects contained in these programmes are varied, they all share the common fundamental methodology upon which the ideas of this book are erected. For having read an early draft of the book and commented upon it, I must record my thanks to Mike Drummond, Alan Maynard, Alan Peacock, Arthur Walker, Alan Williams, Jack Wiseman and Ken Wright. Though they are no longer at York, I must also record my gratitude for the same services rendered by Fritz Grundger and Peter West. Despite their efforts I still fear I have been less articulate, and therefore less persuasive, than I would have liked.

Thanks also to the members of the SSRC-financed Health Economists' Study Group, with whom I have had innumerable pleasant and useful discussions and whose meetings provide such an excellent opportunity not only for trying out half-formed ideas in a sympathetic and helpful environment but also for keeping oneself up to date and for 'feeling the pulse' of health economics in this country.

Mike Cooper, now alas no longer with us in England, also read an early draft and made helpful comments. His own book, *Rationing Health Care*, had a similar intellectual gestation period (though he managed to put pen to paper sooner than I) and is, I think, complementary to mine.

I must also record my grateful thanks to Freda Smith, who typed most of the book, and Barbara Pateman, who helped out when Freda was drowning in a sea of my paper, for their craftmanship and patience.

Finally, I should like to thank in advance those whose work will, in the next few years, round off the rough corners and fill more substance into the gaps of the present work. Within half a decade this book will have become redundant. Such is the pace at which my health economics colleagues are working.

# 1. Introduction

Although the perspective of this book has been much influenced by the author's contact with doctors, epidemiologists, administrators (both academic and practical), operational researchers and policy-makers in Britain and abroad, its perspective remains very much that of the economist. For this no apology is made, because it has been written in the firm belief that there exists no other framework of thought that can at the same time both provide a relevant and thoroughly worked out corpus of analysis through which the problems (sometimes agonising ones) posed by alternative choices can be elucidated, and also, by virtue of this quality, serve as an integrating conception that draws together the other professional and academic disciplines.

The economic approach has been succinctly compared with two others that are frequently found in the literature dealing with the provision — production and allocation — of health care resources by one of the most acute of American health economists, Victor Fuchs:

... the basic economic problem is how to allocate scarce resources so as to best satisfy human wants. This point of view may be contrasted with two others that are frequently encountered. They are the *romantic* and *monotechnic*. The romantic point of view fails to recognize the scarcity of resources relative to wants. The fact that we are constantly being confronted with the need to choose is attributed to capitalism, communism, advertising, the unions, war, unemployment, or any other convenient scapegoat. Because *some* of the barriers to greater output and want satisfaction are clearly man-made, the romantic is misled into confusing the real world with the Garden of Eden. Because it denies the *inevitability* of choice, the romantic point of view is impotent to deal with the basic economic problems that face every society. Occasionally, the romantic point

1

of view is reinforced by authoritarian distinctions between what people 'need' or 'should have'. Confronted with an obvious imbalance between people's desires and the available resources, the romantic—authoritarian response may be to categorize some desires as 'unnecessary' or 'inappropriate', thus protecting the illusion that no scarcity exists.

The monotechnic point of view, frequently found among physicians, engineers, and others trained in the application of a particular technology, is quite different. Its principal limitation is that it fails to recognize the multiplicity of human wants and the diversity of individual preferences. Every problem involving the use of scarce resources has its technological aspects, and the contribution of those skilled in that technology is essential to finding solutions. The solution that is optimal to the engineer or physician, however, may frequently not be optimal for society as a whole because it requires resources that society would rather use for other purposes. The desire of the engineer to build the best bridge or of the physician to practice in the best equipped hospital is understandable. But to the extent that the monotechnic person fails to recognize the claims of competing wants or the divergence of his priorities from those of other people, his advice is likely to be a poor guide to social policy. [Fuchs, 1974]

The NHS has suffered a good deal from the activities of romantics and monotechnics — the former mainly in academic analysis and the latter in the actual running of the service. Too many academic students of the NHS (too few of whom have been economists by training) have tended towards the romantic view to which all sentimental socialists (and who among us is not in some degree a sentimental socialist?) tend, namely that the NHS, with its 'free' health care, is an end in itself rather than a means to an end. On the one hand this has led to an uncritical defence of the NHS (as, e.g., 'the best in the world' — whatever that may mean to whomever), of zero charges to patients and tax finance, and to an assault at every conceivable opportunity on the private sectors of the health industry (whether profit-seeking or not, from the pharmaceutical industry to Nuffield nursing homes); on the other hand its complacency has led to a void as far as real analysis of the NHS's problems is concerned: putting operational content into the word 'need', devising criteria for optimal investment in hospitals and medical manpower, devising criteria for discriminating among the many excessive claimants on the services of the system and so on. Instead, taxonomies and typologies have replaced analysis; detailed description of facts and technologies the application of analysis; and endless discussion of management the analysis of the logical nature of the decisions that have to be made and the implications of that logic for data requirements, the kind of decision-maker required and, hence, administrative structure.

The monotechnics have dominated policy at all levels, from the physician in his surgery who identifies but one symptom at a time (and, from that one symptom, one course of treatment at a time) to senior managers of the system (especially of medical men) who deny the substitutability of various inputs and who refuse (explicitly at least) to face up to the unreality of the views that we must have best practice whatever the cost and that life is of infinite value. Pervading the whole system, there has been the pretence that many problems are financial, management or technical problems, whereas they are often, if only in part, value problems; and the consequence has been that big questions concerning whose are the values that should count have been left unposed and, naturally enough, unanswered. Interestingly, however, there is one form of monotechnism that is relatively absent in the NHS. It seems to be the lot of most publicly owned enterprises to suffer the rigid order imposed upon them by monotechnism, perhaps because its intellectual parents aspire to, or believe they actually have, absolute knowledge. Thus we see, at one time, total commitment to selection by measured IQ in secondary education followed by an equally total commitment to *comprehensive* education; the selection of *one* kind of atomic reactor in electricity generation, and so on. By contrast, decentralisation of decisions about the vast majority of 'techniques', especially in clinical practice, exists in the NHS, and the gradual emergence of a preferred technique is left to the informed scientific judgements of its practitioners. Now, while scientific method precludes our ever taking the intellectually luxurious position of certainty about anything, it is odd that in the more precisely testable areas of medical science monotechnism should be absent, whereas in the extremely risky and uncertain areas of decision-taking such as manpower planning, monotechnism, with its 'all the eggs in one basket' mentality, rules the roost.

As we shall see, there is a role for monotechnism in the NHS, but to understand that role we have to look more closely at the nature of the techniques in question and in particular at the kind of scientific knowledge we possess about the relationship between means and ends. But there can be no place for romanticism. It is only by casting off the intellectual shackles of these two dominant schools of thought that the truly reformatory nature of the economic approach to the NHS, as contrasted with the essential conservatism of the romantic and extreme monotechnic views, will become clear. Many of our implications will not be realisable within twenty years, partly because so much time has been wasted in the prosecution of mostly irrelevant social research into the problems of the NHS and partly because the system has huge political inertia. There are powerful pressure groups both within it and without which would resist reform for self-seeking or romantic ideological (or both) reasons, only some of which can be 'bought off' as Aneurin Bevan 'bought off' the doctors when creating the NHS in the first place.

The root and principal distinguishing mark of an economic approach is its recognition of scarcity of resources on the one hand and the multiplicity of human wants and values on the other. It is simply not true that, if only we were less selfish or greedy, the scarcity problem would disappear. I want better health and education, a better environment, more satisfactory work conditions, more and better food, music and books for myself and my family; but this is not simple materialist 'greed' in the self-indulgent sense we customarily use – I also want more of all these things for others, and this is not selfish. We plainly lack sufficient resources for me and mine to have all we want and for the others to have all we would like them to have. *A fortiori*, we lack sufficient resources for others to have all they want and for still others to have all that the others want for them.

Economists often study the role that prices have in markets, which is that when markets can, or are permitted to, work (even imperfectly), these prices signal the priorities that individuals place upon changes in the distribution of a set of resources in this or that (selfish or unselfish) use. With health care in Britain, money prices have been effectively removed from the consumer's relationship with the system. This may be regarded with approval from a variety of points of view. You may regard the use of money as as medium of exchange between individuals and groups in a society as evil, as a form of Marxian alienation. You may believe that it gives the wrong signals, since the 'strength' of the priority signals each individual gives, if the distribution of money income is unjust, may also be unjust. Or you may believe that, especially in health care, there are collective interests at stake which make it in the interest of all the individuals in that society to remove prices because they are an inappropriate means of indicating the real priorities – the poor man's valuation, as indicated by his spending, of a spell of care in hospital is not the true social valuation, since *I* value his getting care too, and so do you (there is no need to invoke the mysterious argument that the 'State' is somehow independent of its citizens and has preferences of its own that are superior to its citizens' preferences to make this argument against prices).

The removal of prices on the consumer side does, however, pose huge problems for both the fair and the efficient allocation of resources, for they do, at the minimum, indicate an element (even if only part of the picture) in the social value of health care, and the social value of health care is a crucial problem in the NHS. Health care is of infinite value to none of us — we smoke and drink and eat in ways that diminish our health and life expectancy. We play dangerous games and do dangerous jobs. All our daily behaviour denies that we value health infinitely. As taxpayers we reveal the same behaviour: we do not wish taxes so to be increased as to maximise health and, from the taxes we are prepared to pay (some of us more reluctantly than others), we do not wish all to go on health. Some may like to see more spent on health care and less on housing, education, pensions and defence, but no one wants *none* of all these other things. There is no hierarchy of wants: we want more of this and less of that; we don't want *all* of health first, and then, when that is maximised, *all* the education we can possibly get, and so on. In any case, we could easily spend the entire GNP of Britain on the health service — and still want more. So we must choose, both within the health sector, within the public sector and as between public and private. These are the implications of the multiplicity of man's wants in the face of scarcity. How then, in the NHS, can we 'trade off' the advantages of more of 'this' against more of 'that' (in a growing economy), or compare the advantages of more of one thing with the advantage of whatever it is that we shall have to give up (in a static economy)?

Parallel to this willingness (out of necessity) to substitute or choose among wants is the necessity to substitute or choose between the means of meeting the wants — the resources at our disposal. Once again, it is not true that one cannot substitute among health care resources or between them and resources in other sectors of the economy. Substitution, of course, takes time: you cannot convert a teacher into a doctor overnight, or a pre-clinical medical student into an expert surgeon. But the longer the time, the more substitution among resources is possible — and for some maximum substitution can be achieved quite quickly. The question of resource substitution in health has two quite distinct — but all too frequently confused — elements. One of these concerns the *effectiveness* of a combination of resources; the other its *efficiency*. Effectiveness refers, as its name implies, to the effects in terms of outcome of the combination. Other things equal, the *more* outcome, or the higher its quality, the better. Monotechnics among doctors tend to this view — they seek the most effective combination of resources in, say, treating a disease. Efficiency embraces the costs, as well as the effectiveness, of different resource combinations. It recognises that if the resources are used for the proposed purpose then they are not available for some alternative use. The social value of the most preferred of the possible alternatives *is* the cost of the chosen one.

The conflict between effectiveness and efficiency is less apparent if there exist several alternative ways of performing some activity, each of which is equally effective. There the implication is plain: the efficient one is the one with the least cost. More frequently, however, effectiveness is not the same and then we have to begin to ask: is the extra effectiveness of one technique 'worth' the additional cost (supposing it to be more costly)?

It will be clear that the notion of cost to which we are led via our ideas of scarcity and want-multiplicity does not necessarily correspond to the cash expenditures that may be occurred. Indeed, economics teaches us to be as cautious in the interpretation of the money prices of resource inputs such as doctors, beds, nurses, machines and drugs, as it does in the interpretation of prices to consumers of the final service. Thus we may say that the cash paid to doctors *overstates* their real cost since, e.g., we have to pay them that much to stop them all emigrating — but the value of our doctors to, say, North Americans we may choose not to see as a cost *to us in Britain*. Or we may observe that the medical profession is highly monopolised and its training highly subsidised and we may conclude that doctors have succeeded in pushing their incomes above the minimum they need be paid to keep them, in more or less their present numbers, in Britain. In this case their alternative use value, i.e. their true social cost, is less than what they are paid.

An introduction, however, is the wrong place to rely upon controversial examples to sustain interest in a methodological lecture. In the chapters to follow we shall, of course, attempt to put some substantial flesh on to the bones of this analytical approach. Meanwhile, it may be as well to try to dispel the common fear that the cool-headed approach we intend to adopt to the NHS is necessarily associated with a cold heart. It is time to stand up and be counted on what is ultimately an ethical view about the NHS. It is asserted here not because an author has any right to inflict his own value judgements or ethics on his reader but because this author believes that the particular ethical view to be put here is a generally held one among those for whom the NHS exists, viz. all actual and potential patients. The value judgement is this: the fundamental purpose of the NHS, which must be seen as a means rather than an end in itself, is to minimise the extent of ill health in the community. Although this bald and simple statement may seem obvious, it is on closer examination neither so simple nor so obviously desirable as it may appear, for the objective is to be met subject to two crucial sets of constraints: first, the limited amount of resources available, and second, the very nature of man and the fact that his needs and demands are multiple and often themselves conflicting, causing the necessity for *choice*.

The many difficulties that arise of a definitional sort (what *is* ill health in this policy context? what distinguishes 'demand' and 'need'?) and of an operational sort (what effective methods exist within and outside the health services for combating ill health?) will occupy us at some length at various points in the book, but the puzzles posed by the whole conception of minimising ill health will be our continuing concern throughout. One such puzzle concerns the choice of total level of resource availability: we may be able to minimise the level of ill health for any given degree of resource availability, but choosing the appropriate level of resource availability involves us in costing the additional resources and valuing the additional improvement in health — or, as we shall term it, in evaluating *need*. As yet we are not in any position to do this for the entire health sector, in short to decide how large the NHS ought to be; but we shall be able to make some progress at a less highly aggregated level.

A second related difficulty that is not immediately apparent in our bald statement is that the objective does not necessarily imply equality of provision of resources, or of availability, or of the degree to which unmet needs remain in any area. This incompatibility between making the maximum impact on unmet need and egalitarianism, an aspect of a familiar conflict between efficiency and equity in general, will confront us in several guises as we analyse various problems.

The organisation of the book is straightforward. The continuing themes throughout are the various conceptions of need that we have to develop to tackle the problems (for which chapter 2 sets out the general framework) and the necessity for choice among both what services are to be produced and between alternative ways of producing them. Chapter 3 distinguishes the demand for health from the need for health care, emphasising that the demand element is 'objective' or behaviouristic, while the need element is 'subjective' and normative. Chapter 4 takes us further into the business of measuring need and identifies (what is so often fudged or skated over) distinctions between value judgements and other kinds of judgement in the 'needs' notion. This chapter also raises very important questions concerning who should make these value judgements; and since the answer to these questions also requires further value judgements, some are tentatively put forward and discussed. Chapters 5 and 6 introduce the supply side more explicitly and a whole range of choice problems concerning input combinations is discussed. The remainder of the book carries through need, demand and supply together. In chapter 7 the argument about the role of markets in medical care is reviewed. Chapter 8 discusses methods of rationing what supply is available in the NHS. Chapter 9 looks at the regional distribution of need, demand and supply, while chapter 10 extends the territorial comparisons to the international level.

In the last chapter the threads are finally drawn together and some of the principal conclusions are reviewed, together with their principal underpinnings and value assumptions. The latter have been deliberately chosen so as not to be strikingly idiosyncratic or controversial, yet the conclusions that emerge, in their totality, amount to something surprisingly radical if the British NHS is really to fulfil the promises it appears to hold out.

Since the book is about the NHS, relatively little space is devoted to 'alternatives' to the NHS kind of structure: absence of money prices to patients and public ownership of the principal institutions. Indeed, we present several arguments why this structure is indispensable if health services in Britain are to do all for us that they could. There are plenty of other sources to consult for those who wish to explore the alternatives. Likewise, there is no shortage of descriptive and historical material on the NHS. Consequently, the only material of this sort in the book is introduced for quite specific purposes: to identify a problem or elucidate its solution.

Economists working in areas of social policy are frequently accused of 'arrogance', of having 'hot lines to God' and so on. There are few of us of any experience who do not to this day bear the scars of past battles with conservatives, socialists, doctors, administrators. And some scars were doubtless self-inflicted or are the relics of well-deserved trouncings. The attempt has been earnestly made here to distinguish the real contribution of economics, which is to help unravel the often fiendishly complex problems of social choice, from that of other disciplines without which whatever the economist said would be empty.

Thus, for example, we cannot evaluate the purely technical issues of clinical medicine or epidemiology. Likewise, beneath the apparently commonsensical surface of the economist's approach lies a multitude of treacherous traps for the unwary. Some of the difficult issues have, where they are deemed to be mainly of academic and scientific interest, been skipped over (daintily I hope), but others have been explored in more depth.

Economic analysis of health service problems is, however, no game for the amateur. The quack economist is no less a threat to society than the quack doctor. If, then, on some of the biggest issues we sometimes have to remain silent or to pour cold water (and we shall do both!), it will be because the question is the preserve either of other experts or of quacks. If we can do no more however than to indicate the value of the economic approach and to whet the appetite, while making the reader aware that below the surface lies a vast body of highly technical, mostly mathematical, work in the learned journals and scholarly monographs, then our objective will have been attained. Medical policy-making (elsewhere as well as in Britain) has been lumbered for long enough with a baggage train of amateur philosophers, amateur politicians, amateur ideologues, amateur doctors — and amateur economists.

Since, however, the logic of our analysis of the NHS will lead us from the way it is towards a view of how it might be, it is as well to end on the more modest note struck by Augustin Cournot, the great nineteenth century French mathematical economist:

The skill of statesmen ... consists in tempering the ardour of the spirit of innovation, without attempting an impossible struggle against the laws of Providence. Possession of a sound theory may help in this labour of resistance to abrupt changes and assist in easing the transition from one system to another. By giving more light on a debated point it soothes the passions which are aroused. Systems have their fanatics, but the science which succeeds to systems never has them. Finally, even if theories relating to social organizations do not guide the doings of the day, they at least throw light on the history of accomplished facts. Up to a certain point it is possible to compare the influence of economic theories on society to that of grammarians on grammar. Languages are formed without the consent of grammarians, and are corrupted in spite of them; but their works throw light on the laws of the formation and decadence of languages; and their rules hasten the time when a language attains its perfection, and delay a little the invasions of barbarians and bad taste which corrupt it. [quoted by Lord Robbins, *Politics and Economics*, Macmillan, 1963, p. 3]

In an important allegorical sense, an apt subtitle for this book might have been 'a grammar of the NHS'.

## BIBLIOGRAPHY

Cooper, M. H. (1975) *Rationing Health Care* London, Croom Helm; New York, Halstead

Fuchs, V. R. (1974) *Who Shall Live? Health, Economics and Social Choice* New York, Basic Books

Williams, A. and Anderson, R. W. (1975) *Efficiency in the Social Services* London, Basil Blackwell and Martin Robertson

# 2. The Need for Health Care

One of the basic beliefs of the founding fathers of the NHS was that the provision of medical care free of charge would enable the 'backlog' of sickness to be worked off. With the removal of the price barrier, the health service bill would, after an initial period spent working the backlog off, tend to decline as a healty nation became yet healthier. Instead, despite a very modest population growth, the utilisation of health services has, on almost every indicator, increased continuously since the Second World War. Table 2.1 indicates some illustrative dimensions since the mid-1950s. Except where policy has led to the running down of a particular service (as in mass miniature radiography) or where patient charges have been imposed (as for prescriptions), it is exceedingly difficult to find any published statistical series of utilisation that does not display a steady increase.

What is the explanation of this phenomenon? Has demand been increasing continuously? Has need been increasing continuously? Has supply been increasing continuously? If so, what is the explanation? How could the founding fathers have been so wrong? To answer any of these questions sensibly we must begin by inquiring a little more closely into their meaning and how they may interact.

A basic distinction that we shall have to make is between the notion of a person's demand for health as compared with his demand for health care. Clearly, the former is a great deal wider in the factors that it embraces than the latter. For example, the attitude people have towards elements of the environment that affect health (other than health services) such as the food they eat, the sports they engage in,

TABLE 2.1.

*Indicators of health service utilisation*

| | NHS expenditure* as % of GNP (UK) | Hospital discharges and deaths in England and Wales | Courses of dental treatment completed and emergencies in England and Wales | Sight tests given in England and Wales | Bottles of blood issued by National Blood Transfusion Service in England and Wales |
|---|---|---|---|---|---|
| | | ('000) | ('000) | ('000) | ('000) |
| 1956 | 3.6 | 3,739 | 10,658 | 4,927 | |
| 1960 | 3.9 | 4,136 | 13,489 | 5,606 | 900 |
| 1961 | 4.0 | 4,269 | 14,337 | 5,549 | 948 |
| 1962 | 4.0 | 4,391 | 15,020 | 5,440 | 981 |
| 1963 | 4.0 | 4,576 | 16,065 | 5,569 | 1,024 |
| 1964 | 4.0 | 4,725 | 17,067 | 5,950 | 1,090 |
| 1965 | 4.1 | 4,818 | 17,692 | 6,115 | 1,131 |
| 1966 | 4.3 | 4,898 | 18,430 | 6,213 | 1,181 |
| 1967 | 4.5 | 5,012 | 19,411 | 6,451 | 1,225 |
| 1968 | 4.6 | 5,150 | 20,066 | 6,633 | 1,274 |
| 1969 | 4.6† | 5,282 | 20,226 | 6,722 | 1,303 |
| 1970 | 4.8 | 5,329 | 20,748 | 6,767 | 1,303 |
| 1971 | 4.9 | 5,494 | 22,038 | 6,831 | |
| 1972 | 5.1 | 5,550 | 23,418 | 6,897 | |
| 1973 | 4.9 | 5,452 | 24,756 | 7,293 | |

*Includes fees paid by NHS patients.
†From 1969, some local authority services were transferred from NHS to social services.

their enthusiasm for personal and household hygiene, the extent to which they smoke, drink, stay up late and so on all *reflect* a person's demand for health and, in turn, *affect* his demand for health care services. We shall return to this distinction later in the next chapter.

The notion of 'need', by contrast, seems in all its conventional uses to refer to a need for health care services rather than a need for any particular level of health *per se*. Upon reflection, however, it would seem to be sensible to regard the need for health care services as ultimately related to a need for health *per se*, since it seems not unrealistic to suppose that health services are best viewed as instrumental in the promotion of better health.

Unfortunately, it is not possible even to infer this much from much of the policy discussion that uses the word 'need' in the context of planning or setting objectives for the NHS. A few illustrative quotations illustrate the confusion that confronts us (and the policy-makers):

There are some needs which cannot be self-diagnosed; for medical care, for instance, or mental health services or rehabilitation services. There are some needs which, though they are 'felt' needs, are not expressed because of ignorance on the part of the individual that services exist, and that anything can be done to mitigate or remove the need . . . . There are . . . many systems of rationing or barriers which operate to deter the expression of need . . . . [T] he poor, the badly educated, the old, those living alone and other handicapped groups . . . are often the people with the greatest needs. [Titmuss, 1968, p. 66]

*Normative need* is that which the expert or professional, administrator or social scientist defines as need in any given situation. A 'desirable' standard is laid down. . . . [*Felt need*] is equated with want. When assessing the need for a service, the population is asked whether they feel they need it . . . . *Expressed need* or demand is felt need turned into action . . . . *Comparative need* is obtained by studying the characteristics of the population in receipt of a service. If there are people with similar characteristics not in receipt of a service, then they are in need. [Bradshaw, 1972, pp. 72–3; my italics]

A need for medical care exists when an individual has an illness or disability for which there is an effective and acceptable treatment or cure. [Matthew, 1971, p. 27]

'Needs' are those demands which in the opinion of the doctor require medical attention. That is, they are an expert's view of our health state. [Cooper, 1975, p. 20]

The aim of the programme is to provide, within the resources available, a full range of health and personal social services for all those in need of them . . . the basic objectives will continue to be to meet health or social needs wherever and whenever they arise. . . . [H.M. Treasury, 1973, p. 98]

The aim of the programme is to provide within the resources available, health and personal social services for the whole population, with particular emphasis on helping people who have special needs, such as the elderly, the mentally ill and handicapped and the young . . . [and] . . . to ensure that the services available in any area are more closely related to its particular needs. . . . [H.M. Treasury, 1975, p. 104]

. . . the word 'need' ought to be banished from discussion of public policy, partly because of its ambiguity but also because . . . in many public discussions it is difficult to tell, when someone says that 'society needs . . .', whether he means that *he* needs it, whether he means that society ought to get it in *his* opinion, whether a *majority* of the members of society want it, or *all* of them want it. Nor is it clear whether it is 'needed' *regardless* of the cost to society. [Culyer *et al*, 1972]

The one thing (and it is just about the only thing) that each of the definitions or implied definitions in these quotations have in common is that the need spoken about is a need for a service. As Alan Williams points out in a highly perceptive discussion of 'needology' (Williams, 1974), quoting Barry (1965) in support, the question is an evaluative, normative one and must relate, ultimately, to the *end* being sought and to which the services in question are *instrumental means.* The choice among these latter (e.g. more or fewer hospital beds; particular surgical or medical interventions) is, or should be, mainly a technical and economic matter: they are 'needed' only in so far as the end or outcome of the use is needed. One of the principal dangers of the language of 'needology' applied to instruments is that it encourages a particular form of sloppy thinking, namely a denial of the substitutability of alternative means in attaining an end or, at least, a denial of the legitimacy of considering that the most effective means of meeting an ultimate need may be 'too' costly and that possibly to adopt a less effective means, or a less comprehensive means, or indeed no means at all might be the proper course.

The importance of the effective instrumentality of health services can scarcely be over-emphasised. Indeed we shall devote the whole of one of the following chapters to it. For our present purposes, however, it suffices to note that the 'need' for services in this sense is in principle a technical matter which, while in practice is not devoid of the necessity for making judgements, does not require the making of *value* judgements about the ultimate needs of individuals. It is also striking that only one of the above quotations (which are a rather representative sample of conventional usage) approaches anything like the conception of technical need — a necessary means to an end. This one exception is Dr Matthew's view that a need exists only when 'there is an effective and acceptable treatment or cure'. But the great limitation of this definition is that it implies that a need does not exist where no effective and acceptable treatment or cure exists. Even without inquiring into what 'effective' and 'acceptable' might mean, the definition is plainly unsatisfactory, since it is not meaningless to talk about an individual 'needing' a treatment that may not exist at all. But even as a technical definition it is unsatisfactory, since usually more than one 'effective and acceptable' treatment is available if any is available at all, as we shall see in greater detail later on. And since this is the case, we have to ask which of the alternatives is needed. A little reflection on this question should rapidly convince the reader that this conception of 'need' is not particularly helpful to anyone who may be engaged in deciding what services in general or particular ought to be provided.

Implicit in the definitions we have listed is another common quality: one has the feeling that somewhere a third party is doing some evaluation. From Professor Titmuss's quotation we may infer that, since many of the most important needs are not expressed by those in need, they must be being expressed by someone else (in the limit, if only by Professor Titmuss). Although Jonathan Bradshaw allows one kind of need to be identified with 'want', this is not a very helpful equation since there are lots of 'wants' that everyone will agree are not in any sense 'needed', and in any case we already have the word 'want' in the vocabulary. But his concept of 'normative need' clearly identifies some third parties — the experts and professionals. Similarly, Michael Cooper identifies the third party in the NHS as presently organised as medical practitioners, which requires the individuals who may be designated as 'in need' also to 'demand' some service, which denies the possibility of Titmussian need, where the individuals in question may not demand anything but nevertheless be seen by others as 'in need'. Since Cooper's portrayal of the present nature of need as the system recognises it is very persuasive, the incompleteness of the kind of 'needs' actually considered in the NHS is plain. The first Treasury quotation is remarkable for its sublime emptiness of any real content at all while the second seems again to imply the exercise of a third party's judgement about which client groups 'need' services.

The existence of this shadow in the wings is, as it turns out, quite crucial for a clear conception of the need for health care and, indeed, for a proper understanding of health service organisation and planning. At the most general level, the shadow in the wings is you and me. If we think that someone else 'needs' some service then, so far as we are concerned, he needs it and we are expressing, in a kind of shorthand, our view that 'something' *ought to be done* to change his health status. It would be silly for most of us to pretend to know what that something should be, but we can and do express the view that the somebody else in question (which may in practice be wide client groups such as mothers-to-be, or old persons, or cancer victims, or 'the British people') ought to be healthier than they are, or ought to be protected from potential health hazards. Does the individual dying of thirst in the desert 'need' a glass of water? Technically, yes, if he is to live.

Normatively, yes only if others agree he ought to have it. If they do not, he may *want* it as much as it is possible to want anything, but he does not, on our definition, need it.

At more specific levels, the 'shadow in the wings' may be a health service minister, or administrator, or a doctor, nurse, etc.

What does this conception of need as being determined crucially by the judgement of a third party imply? First, and most obviously, it raises the question of which third parties should have their judgements legitimised in the health care system — the public, experts, economists, social workers, doctors, administrators, politicians? If each is to have a legitimate role in the defining of need, what is that role to be?

Second, our definition does not imply that need is *absolute*. Just as we have already suggested that the technical concept of need as the selection of an appropriate means towards a given end is not absolute, for several means usually exist and a choice has to be made, so it is crucial to be aware of the fact that need for care is itself also a variable. This is an empirical fact: people's views about what others need depend upon a whole variety of factors, deriving from the prevailing culture and social philosophy of a society. The particular contribution that economics can make, however, derives from the proposition that the degree to which any given need will be met will also depend upon the costs of meeting it. It just happens to be the fact that, the greater the cost becomes of meeting a given need, the less will that need be met.

The non-absoluteness of need for health also follows as a matter of normative logic from the notion of need itself. Plainly, individuals are regarded as being in need of many things other than health services to improve their health status: they need education, housing, legal protection, food, etc., etc. The need for any one of these things cannot be treated as logically independent of the rest because the meeting of needs requires the using up of some of the resources available to a society and these are strictly limited. We are forced to rank needs, to assess and to reassess priorities as resource availability changes through economic growth or decline or as the relative costs of meeting needs change for technical reasons. If it is discovered that we can educate our children no worse by having, say, larger classes, then *all* our priorities may be reassessed: instead of training and paying some future teachers, we may improve the capital stock of schools and/or train more nurses and/or build more council houses and/or employ more policemen. Thus, we must of necessity choose from among those moral things we think we ought to do in order to devise the best 'package' in light of what is possible. Of necessity, this requires us to trade off one need against the other. Not only, therefore, *do* we do this trading off, but it is also logically inescapable and, ethically, completely legitimate.

Our definition of need thus implies the necessity of choice as to arbiter of need. In turn, the arbiters must choose between rival needs and decide how much of each will be met. A third implication of our definition is that, if need is indeed subject to definition only by a third party, a party external to the individual in need, there must exist some indicator, some observable characteristics, that inheres in the individual and can be taken by the third party as conveying to him the basic information he requires in order to assess whether or not a person is to be regarded (by him) as being in need.

Essentially, it is this interpretation of the meaning of 'need' and its implications that concern us in the rest of this book. The precise nature of these indicators will be the principal theme of most of our subsequent discussion, and in the course of developing it many of the questions concerning justice and equity in health service arrangements, which have so dominated academic inquiry, will be met again. Not least of the advantages of the approach here is that it makes possible a much more comprehensive treatment of the issues as well as indicating how they may be considered and incorporated into planning practice. Economists' traditional treatments of matters concerning distributive justice have in the past focused far too obsessively upon the personal income distribution, this in turn, probably because economists have usually failed to pay more than lip service to the essential duality of man, focusing upon man as a productive agent and less — much less — upon man as the ultimate end of economic activity and social organisation (Culyer and Wiseman, 1975). Full recognition of the duality of man, however, forces us, both for prediction and prescription, to go well beyond the rather arid and formal specification of 'utility' functions of the usual sort in economics. In particular, in the present context it takes us into the treacherous territory of 'need' and, while not requiring us to jettison the traditional tools of economic analysis, it does require the forging of new ones to enable us to tackle the problems exposed by the wider vistas offered if the notion of duality is taken seriously.

## BIBLIOGRAPHY

Barry, B. (1965) *Political Argument* London, Routledge and Kegan Paul

Boulding, K. E. (1966) 'The Concept of Need for Health Services' *Milbank Memorial Fund Quarterly*, vol. 44

Bradshaw, J. S. (1972) 'A Taxonomy of Social Need' in McLachlan (1972)

Cooper, M. H. (1975) *Rationing Health Care* London, Croom Helm

Culyer, A. J., Lavers, R. J. and Williams, Alan (1972) 'Health Indicators' in Shonfield and Shaw (1972)

Culyer, A. J. (ed.) (1974) *Economic Policies and Social Goals: Aspects of Public Choice* London, Martin Robertson

Culyer, A. J. and Wiseman, J. (1975) 'Public Economics and the Concept of Human Resources', paper given at the 31st Congress of the International Institute of Public Finance at Nice, September 1975

H. M. Treasury (1973) *Public Expenditure to 1977—78* Cmnd. 5519, London, HMSO

H. M. Treasury (1975) *Public Expenditure to 1978—79* Cmnd. 5879, London, HMSO

McLachlan, G. (1971) *Portfolio for Health* London, Oxford University Press

McLachlan, G. (1972) *Problems and Progress in Medical Care, Essays on Current Research, Seventh Series* London, Oxford University Press

Matthew, G. K. (1971) 'Measuring Need and Evaluating Services' in McLachlan (1971)

Shonfield, A. and Shaw, S. (1972) *Social Indicators and Social Policy* London, Heinemann

Titmuss, R. M. (1968) *Commitment to Welfare* London, Allen and Unwin

Williams, Alan (1974) ' "Need" as a Demand Concept (with Special Reference to Health)' in Culyer (1974)

# 3. The Demand for Health Care

A major conclusion of chapter 2 was that the need for health care is defined by reference to some third party's view as to what a particular individual or class of individuals *ought* to receive. The demand for health care, however, is indicated by the individuals themselves in making claims upon health care resources. As such, it may be influenced by prevailing notions of need (through education or pressure group activities) but will also be influenced by the income of the persons concerned, the prices they confront, their level of educational attainment and many other factors, including, of course, their state of health. Indeed, as we shall see later in this chapter, there is much to be gained from viewing the demand for health care as being derived from an underlying and more fundamental *demand for health* itself, which will embrace demands for all health affecting entities in society, such as environmental factors, housing and nutrition as well as the health care services provided by the NHS and the private sector (including chemists' non-prescription sales and 'health' foods as well as private medical care).

A first and very important fact to bear in mind is that not all those who are, in clinical terms, 'sick' demand medical care, even when it is available free of money charges. An early attempt to identify the magnitude of the so-called submerged 'iceberg' of sickness found in the late 1930s that over 90 per cent of more than 3,000 people examined had some identifiable sickness but only 26 per cent were aware of being sick (and hence capable of expressing a potential demand) and, of these, only 8 per cent had been receiving medical attention. Table 3.1

TABLE 3.1.

*The clinical iceberg: England and Wales 1962*

|  |  | No. of recognised sufferers ('000) | Estimated total no. of cases ('000) | Cases in which no treatment was being sought ('000) |
|---|---|---|---|---|
| Hypertension | males 45+ | 170 | 620 | 450 |
|  | females 45+ | 500 | 2,720 | 2,220 |
| Urinary infections | females 15+ | 420 | 830 | 410 |
| Glaucoma | aged 45+ | 60 | 340 | 280 |
| Epilepsy |  | 160 | 280 | 120 |
| Rheumatoid arthritis | aged 15+ | 230 | 520 | 290 |
| Psychiatric disorders | males 15+ | 560 | 1,200 | 640 |
|  | females 15+ | 1,290 | 2,120 | 830 |
| Diabetes mellitus |  | 290 | 600 | 310 |
| Bronchitis | males 45−64 | 500 | 980 | 480 |
|  | females 45−64 | 390 | 500 | 110 |

*Source:* Office of Health Economics, *New Frontiers in Health* London, OHE (1964).

shows the estimated number of untreated instances of a selection of treatable cases in 1962.

More comprehensive information about morbidity and untreated sickness is likely, in the future, to be obtained from the General Household Survey. This inquires (among other things) about whether individuals in the sample have recently been restricted in their normal activity owing to sickness, and it has two great advantages in that it provides a data source that is independent of GP and hospital records and that sickness can be related to other socio-economic measures of the status of individuals. Table 3.2 gives the percentage of the average rate of sickness by diagnostic category. In all cases (except for eye disease) it can be seen that semi- and unskilled manual workers have a substantially higher incidence of sickness than any other social class. In general, too, the pattern is clear: the lower down the socio-economic scale one goes, the higher the incidence of sickness. What is also striking is the differential in the utilisation of services: professional and

## TABLE 3.2.

*Variations in the average rate of sickness and GP consultations per 1,000 population causing limited long-standing illness by socio-economic group (males only), England and Wales, 1971*

| Condition | Average rate per 1,000 | Percentage of average | | | |
|---|---|---|---|---|---|
| | | Professional, employers and managers | Intermediate and junior non-manual | Skilled manual | Semi-skilled and unskilled manual |
| Mental disorders | 11.0 | 59 | 65 | 95 | 175 |
| Diseases of nervous system | 8.7 | 75 | 87 | 79 | 156 |
| Diseases of eye | 7.3 | 97 | 112 | 77 | 105 |
| Diseases of ear | 7.7 | 56 | 70 | 110 | 142 |
| Heart disease | 24.4 | 83 | 91 | 85 | 141 |
| Other circulatory diseases | 10.5 | 85 | 70 | 86 | 150 |
| Bronchitis | 16.9 | 47 | 69 | 106 | 167 |
| Other low respiratory diseases | 13.5 | 78 | 96 | 93 | 141 |
| Diseases of digestive system | 11.4 | 71 | 78 | 101 | 148 |
| Arthritis and rheumatism | 27.5 | 73 | 90 | 79 | 161 |
| Other diseases of musculoskeletal system | 9.3 | 76 | 101 | 99 | 122 |
| Fractures etc. | 6.3 | 67 | 57 | 105 | 170 |
| Other injuries | 9.5 | 59 | 102 | 100 | 146 |
| Consultations per person per year | 3.1 | 100 | 97 | 103 | 113 |

*Source:* Tables 8.13 and 8.36 in *The General Household Survey – Introductory Report* London, HMSO (1973)

managerial persons, who have about three-quarters of the average incidence of sickness, have an average consultation rate; unskilled and semi-skilled persons, whose average incidence is over half as much again as the average, consult only a little more frequently than average.

Two questions suggest themselves. First, is there not some social injustice here and, if so, what should be done about it? Second, why is this so? In Britain, health care treatment is free of money charges, so why should those who are, on the whole, poorer appear to demand less than one would predict simply on the basis of the incidence of disease?

Now, if our answer to the first part of the first question is: yes, there is social injustice here or, less strongly, we should seek to raise the health status of the lower socio-economic groups, the answer to the second part of the question (concerning what should be done) will depend at least in part upon the factors determining (i) the relatively low health status of the lower socio-economic groups and (ii) the factors determining their utilisation of health services. (The 'in part' is there because it is possible that the explanation may depend also upon the way in which services are supplied. For example, doctors may discriminate in some ways against the lower social groups.)

The factors determining both health status and utilisation of health services are, together, to be seen as determining the *demand for health itself*. On the face of it, the basic problem we have to explain is why the lower social classes in general seem to have a lower demand for health than the higher classes. This shows most dramatically, of course, in mortality rates. Table 3.3 shows the age-specific male death rates in England and Wales for 1951 and 1961.

We see from this table that our general inferences about morbidity (the prevalence of sickness) are confirmed by statistics of mortality: in both 1951 and 1961 mortality rates were lower for persons in social class 1 than in social class 5. Moreover, for those aged fifty-five and over in social class 5, the mortality rate actually rose over this period!

Even in the United States, where one may be tempted to conclude that financial barriers to health care would explain higher morbidity and mortality among lower social classes, it is clear that, while financial factors do play *some* role, they are by no means the *whole* explanation. Thus a study of patients in the pre-paid Kaiser Permanente plan in California — with free health care on demand — found higher blood pressures associated with lower social class (Oakes and Syme, 1973). A study in Boston of cancer patient survival showed lower survival rates

TABLE 3.3.

*Age-specific male death rates per 100,000 population in England and Wales, 1951 and 1961*

| Age group | Social class 1 | | Social class 5 | |
|---|---|---|---|---|
| | 1951 | 1961 | 1951 | 1961 |
| 25–34 | 162 | 76 | 214 | 179 |
| 35–44 | 230 | 165 | 386 | 381 |
| 45–54 | 756 | 528 | 1,027 | 1,010 |
| 55–64 | 2,347 | 1,765 | 2,567 | 2,716 |
| 65–69 | 4,839 | 4,004 | 4,868 | 5,142 |
| 70–74 | 7,614 | 6,278 | 7,631 | 8,390 |

*Source:* D. Butler and D. Stokes, *Political Change in Britain: Forces Shaping Electoral Choice* Macmillan, London, (1969), p. 265, footnote 1.

among lower-income groups (Lipworth *et al.*, 1970). In neither case could the explanation be that these patients failed to receive care or that they received systematically inferior quality care (as measured by the quality or quantity of the inputs) — indeed, the lower social groups tended to receive more care).

A thoroughgoing answer to the question 'why do people become ill?' clearly depends upon a complexity of factors, many of which are, at present, poorly understood. At root there is, of course, the clinical problem of aetiology which can identify *a* cause of (say) tuberculosis as the result of an attack of the tubercle bacillus on the host but does not as yet explain satisfactorily why different hosts have a different ability to withstand attacks of equal virulence (Dubos and Dubos, 1952): the bacillus is a necessary but not sufficient condition for sickness. Or, why is it that, while a higher proportion of smokers than non-smokers contract lung cancer, many smokers do not contract it and some non-smokers do — perhaps smoking is neither a necessary *nor* a sufficient condition for this disease?

The demand for health, or the economics of aetiology, is of course an extremely young newcomer among its longer standing demographic and epidemiological brethren, but as the demographers and epidemiologists increasingly see the need for a broader approach to the problems of disease in society, so economics (and sociology) begin to be drawn in as behavioural disciplines with every possibility of widening the range of useful hypotheses to be tested in seeking the fundamental causes of disease incidence and prevalence. The 'economics of aetiology' can never, of course, provide a complete explanation, and since this approach is only now beginning to be explored, it is too early yet to decide whether it even has a net contribution to make to our understanding. In the remainder of this chapter we outline what the approach entails.

The demand for health itself is a demand for an investment good — one that yields services over a period of time. These services fall basically into two classes: the direct 'utility' of feeling well on the one hand and, on the other, the indirect benefits derived from an increased amount of healthy time available for productive use both at work (increasing money income) and in non-work activity (household work, leisure activities, etc.) which increases the productivity with which purchased goods and services are used to produce more ultimate sources of utility (an example: higher money income increases the ability to buy fillet steak and wine for home consumption; more healthy time at home increases opportunities to combine these, by studying and practising cooking, into the more ultimate good, a meal, and affords more time in which the meal may be enjoyed — perhaps with friends).

At any moment an individual 'owns' a particular stock of health which is subject to depreciation as time passes and which, if depreciation goes far enough, falls low enough to result in death. Like other capital goods, the stock of health can usually be increased by investment. The relationship between investment and the stock of health for any individual can be regarded as dependent upon the amount of time and money he devotes to improving the stock. Key variables here include diet, exercise, housing, consumption habits and environmental factors such as public health provision (cleanliness of water supplies, efficiency of waste disposal, etc.) and education — health education and general educated common sense obviously affect the efficiency with which the other inputs in the production function are put together. Finally, an important input is, of course, consumption of medical care.

To a greater or lesser extent, these variables are under the control of the individual. Some are barely controllable, such as the existence of some disease-inducing microscopic organisms whose behavioural characteristics are not well understood. Some may be effectively controllable only through the *collective* action of individuals (for example, immunisation against communicable disease or quarantine arrangements). Others are controllable at the individual level (diet, exercise, personal cleanliness, education, etc.). To the extent that some variables are under the control of the individual, he may be regarded as *choosing* his preferred stock of health, or rate of investment, subject, of course, to constraints that are principally the amount of time available to him in total, the way he divides it between work and non-work activity, and the value of his time in work (viz. his wage).

By using a familiar proposition of economics — the higher the cost, the less in any time period will the activity be chosen whose cost has risen — several important implications can be derived which enable us to go a substantial way both in explaining the phenomena we have already observed and in predicting others.

Beyond a certain age it is the case that the rate of biological depreciation of the stock of health is positively correlated with age. This implies that the cost of maintaining the stock of health rises. If all else remains the same, the demand theorem predicts that a lower stock will be chosen. Thus, one would predict that as people become older, after standardising for sex, income, etc., they would also become less healthy: quite independently of the fact that unavoidable and irreversible deterioration of health may occur, there will be additional deterioration.

What will be the effect of rising wages? Higher rates of pay have two effects: on the one hand they increase the value of healthy time, since they make more consumption possible and consumption takes time; on the other hand the cost of time in the health production function also rises. The former tends to encourage investment in health, the latter to discourage it. Which effect will dominate? So long as time is not the *only* input in the health production function (which it usually is not), one would expect the former effect to dominate if all other factors remain the same, since the ratio of benefits to costs of investment in health will rise. Hence, if people are the same in all other respects, we would expect those with higher earned incomes to be healthier: they would tend both to consume more health-promoting inputs (since their cost per unit of time is lower), to spend more time on health-promoting activities and, in general, to be less sick.

One complication worth noting at this point is that some forms of consumption that are harmful to health increase as income increases. If, as one becomes richer, one smokes more, eats too much, consumes more alcohol and drives faster cars, we may find that health and real wage rates are inversely related. This effect seems to help account for the differences that have been observed between longitudinal evidence of income and health and cross-sectional evidence. Through time, as individuals' real wages rise, they tend not to change their consumption habits very dramatically. But if one compares countries that have widely varying income levels in a particular year, one observes quite dramatic differences in consumption habits, with high-income—high-consumption societies having substantially higher mortality rates from certain consumption-related causes of death such as suicide, motorcar accidents, cirrhosis of the liver and lung cancer, than low-income—low-consumption societies. On the other hand, as low-income societies become richer they tend to become healthier, at least up to the point at which the consumption effects begin to dominate the other effects that tend to promote better health.

Education, as we have observed above, tends to improve health. This happens in three ways. On the one hand, better educated persons tend to be better informed persons and better informed persons tend to know more about effects of consumption forms that are hazardous to health (the statistical association between smoking and lung cancer had a dramatic effect on doctors' smoking habits and subsequently a much greater impact on the smoking habits of the better educated members of society than on those of the less well educated members). The second effect operates directly in the health production function by increasing the efficiency with which health-promoting inputs are combined together. The third effect operates via the association between education and the productivity of working time, which raises real wages, which, as we have already seen, on balance increases the demand for health.

We should again, perhaps, note a complication. Increases in the demand for health are not always associated with increases in the demand for medical care. For example, improved education may raise the productivity of inputs in health production function *other than* medical care and thus cause some substitution *away from* health service consumption. Conversely, decreases in the demand for health may cause increases in the demand for care (especially if mediated by a third party). For example, self-poisonings, which are showing a disturbing upward trend for all ages and sexes, are increasingly using up hospital resources.

Statistical support for some of these propositions is presented in table 3.4, which shows the percentage effect on mortality of a ten per cent change in four major health-affecting variables. This cross-sectional study (for the USA) suggests that the high income elasticity of some

TABLE 3.4.

*Percent changes in US age-specific mortality rates resulting from a 10 per cent increase in several variables*

|  | | 10% increase in: | | Per capita health expenditure |
|---|---|---|---|---|
|  | Income | Education | Cigarette consumption | |
| % change in mortality | +2.0 | −2.2 | +1.0 | −0.65 |

*Source:* R. Auster *et al.,* 'The Production of Health; an exploratory study' in V. Fuchs (ed) *Essays in the Economics of Health and Medical Care* New York, NBER Columbia University Press (1972), table 8.3, p. 145.

consumption patterns that are harmful to health are, in the United States, dominating other effects tending in the opposite direction. Cigarette consumption has the expected sign, as have education (years of schooling) and health care expenditures. It is noticeable that either a ten per cent increase in education or a ten per cent reduction in smoking would both have a greater impact on the population's health status, as measured by age-specific mortality rates, than a ten per cent increase in real health care expenditures. This relatively small *marginal* impact of health services on health in wealthy countries is something to which we shall return later.

The importance of focusing on the demand for health at a broad level rather than only on the demand for health care has many insights to offer, of which only a few major ones can be here examined. Another set of interesting implications, which are surely not too fanciful, relates to the complementarity between the demand for health and the demand for other dimensions of the good life which require healthy time to be available if they are to be enjoyed to the full. For example, it has been widely noted that the age-adjusted mortality rates for widowed and divorced men are much higher than for married men or young bachelors. It is surely not implausible to suppose that this is because they lack some other dimensions of the good life that make good health valuable. If our theory about the demand for health is true, we would expect this mortality differential to be mainly accounted for by causes of death in which individual choice of health stock is plainly possible. And indeed this is the case: death rates for the widowed and divorced men are much higher from suicide, motor accidents, cirrhosis of the liver and lung cancer, where 'choice' is more possible, than from vascular lesions, diabetes or cancer of the digestive organs, where it is less possible or where, at least, the relationship between life-style and health states is more obscure. Married persons generally have better health and live longer. In addition to this 'demand' effect, there may also be a 'production' effect: good health tends to be produced more efficiently in a marriage or with cohabitation, where partners can specialise in household life according to their various relative productivities.

In this discussion we seem to have moved a good deal away from the simple concern of earlier economists with money prices, insurance and the demand for health services. In later chapters, we shall look in more detail at some of the issues raised, for example, by the debate about the role of the market in health care provision, but meanwhile our present emphasis is surely right — the price of a thing is not only the money you must pay to get it; the demand for a thing is not independent of demands for other things; the determinants of the stock of health are clearly many. And if we have only begun to scratch the surface we can at least see how economics, demography and epidemiology begin to link together and also, with the great advantage of hindsight, we can see how naive were the views of the founding fathers of the NHS. Free medical care did not (and could not) bring about the abolition of the 'backlog' of sickness. 'To each according to his need for health care' is a largely empty slogan in a free society. Why so? Simply because, even if we could agree what was 'needed', whether a person gets what he needs depends upon his *demand* for health, and even if we were able to standardise for everything else (housing, environment, income and so on) we would still find that the inherent value placed upon good health would vary among individuals.

The great policy issue for the NHS still remains with us: how, specifically, shall we decide who needs what, and how in a free society (i.e. without compulsion) are we to get individuals to express what we see to be a need as *their demand for* health care? And now we have complicated it still further. Since it should evidently be a person's health status in which we are interested, rather than his health care consumption, how do we set about measuring this and how do we set about choosing from among all of those factors that we know affect status, only one of which is medical care? In short, if we do not 'operate' on the patient, upon what other factors, or combination of factors that affect health, should we operate?

## BIBLIOGRAPHY

Anderson, O. (1958) 'Infant Mortality and Social and Cultural Factors – historical trends and current patterns' in E. G. Jaco (ed.) *Patients, Physicians and Illness* New York, Free Press

Auster, R., Leveson, I. and Sarachek, D. (1972) 'The Production of Health: an exploratory study' in V. R. Fuchs (ed.) *Essays in the Economics of Health and Medical Care* New York and London, Columbia University Press

Benjamin, B. (1965) *Social and Economic Factors Affecting Mortality* The Hague, Mouton

Dubos, R. and Dubos, J. (1952) *The White Plague: tuberculosis man and society* Boston, Little, Brown and Co

Fuchs, V. R. (1972) 'The Contribution of Health Services to the American Economy' in Fuchs (ed.) *Essays in the Economics of Health and Medical Care* New York, Columbia University Press

Grossman, M. (1972) *The Demand for Health: a theoretical and empirical investigation* New York and London, Columbia University Press

Kadushin, C. (1964) 'Social Class and the Experiences of Ill-health' *Sociological Inquiry*, vol. 34

Lipworth, L., Abelin, T. and Connelly, R. R. (1970) 'Socio-economic Factors in the Prognosis of Cancer Patients' *Journal of Chronic Diseases*, vol. 23

Mechanic, D. (1968) *Medical Sociology: a selective view* London, Collier Macmillan

Morris, J. N. (1964) *The Uses of Epidemiology* Edinburgh, E. and S. Livingstone

Morris, J. N. and Heady, J. A. (1955) 'Social and Biological Factors in Infant Mortality' *Lancet* (i)

Oakes, T. W. and Syme, S. L. (1973) 'Social Factors in Newly Discovered Elevated Blood Pressure' *Journal of Health and Social Behaviour*, vol. 14.

Rein, M. (1969) 'Social Class and the Utilization of Medical Care Services: A Study of British Experience under the National Health Service' *Hospitals*, 1 July

Steward, W. H. and Enterline, P. (1961) 'Effects of the National Health Service on Physician Utilization and Health in England and Wales' *New England Journal of Medicine*, vol. 265

Strauss, A. L. (1969) 'Medical Organization, Medical Care and Lower Income Groups' *Social Science and Medicine*, vol. 3

Susser, M. W. and Watson, W. (1962) *Sociology in Medicine* London, Oxford University Press

Townsend, P. (1974) 'Inequality and the Health Service' *Lancet*, 15 June

# 4. Measuring Health : the First Step in Need Evaluation

The concept of need as developed in this book up to the present point is (a) an assessment by a third party or parties of (b) an individual's, group's or population's health status such that (c) it ought to be increased. It remains to identify the third party or parties, to define the meaning of health status, to explore the nature of the value judgements involved in both these procedures, and to devise a means for comparing needs individually and by group and a means for comparing needs with the costs of meeting them. Whether a need is to be met will depend upon the value judgements, upon the technical possibilities available and upon the costs of doing so. In each of these senses our concept of need is 'relative': the 'ought' in the expression 'needs ought to be met' is highly conditional.

In this chapter the first major step towards the development of an operational concept of need is taken. We devise a measure of health status, examine its possible uses, explore the value judgements inherent in any measure of health status and suggest the roles in making these value judgements that are appropriate for patients on the one hand and third parties on the other.

Imagine, for the moment, that you are a neurosurgeon treating patients suffering severe head injuries such as may follow, for example, from a motorcar accident. Since the resources at your command both for the immediate treatment of a patient in trauma and for his subsequent care

are, alas, limited the question of (i) which resources you will seek to have, (ii) how you will use them and (iii) to which patients you will give what will depend — though not exclusively — on the success with which you expect your resuscitation, surgery, intensive and nursing care to improve patients' conditions: in short, not merely on whether or not he survives, but also on the quality of survival. At present the conventions are to use rather casual language to describe patient states through time and to give detail to a prognosis; for example, one report of recovery after traumatic decerebration included among 'excellent' recoveries some patients with residual hemiplegia (paralysis of one side of the body) or dysphagia (difficulty with swallowing), while some among 'good' recoveries included 'needed help to walk across the room'. But if you seek something more you get into deep water.

A patient may make a good physical recovery but undergo a personality change. If mental disability does result it may be hard to observe: psychometric testing is limited largely to measuring cognitive skills, and clear organic dementia (i.e. feeble-mindedness owing to brain damage) may go underestimated because a patient's euphoria will often lead him to underplay his disability. Subsequently, the patient will recall how well he was before the injury and become depressed (along with his family, perhaps) by having to accept permanent disabilities.

How then can one devise a measure of the health status of such patients? Its value would be immense, not only in monitoring the patient's condition and supplying him with the appropriate care, but in comparing the impact of alternative clinical procedures upon patient state in some detail, and also in correlating future states of health with early symptomatic measures taken from the patient in trauma, or shortly after, in order to identify those symptoms that indicate favourable prognoses and, hence, the selection of patients for treatment who have reasonable chances of 'recovery'.

Alternatively, suppose now that you are the person responsible for allocating help to the elderly in your area. What kind of help would be appropriate to which people? The criterion of need might well boil down to a few major areas of human activity such as sensory perception, intellectual functioning, physical mobility and the ability to care for oneself. But how would you measure these and, subsequently, combine them into an overall measure of severity of need for any given individual so as to enable you to decide, for example, whether they would be better off in a welfare home or would be no worse off at home with domiciliary support of various kinds?

Again, suppose you are a hospital consultant in general surgery concerned with assigning your 'cold' surgery patients (i.e. those whose condition will not markedly deteriorate without immediate surgery) an order of priority on the waiting list. Clearly, a part of your judgement about when the patient should be admitted will depend upon how fast you expect the condition to deteriorate and what additional complications may set in. But should it not also include the pain and mental anguish the patient may be suffering, whether or not he or she is able to work, whether he or she has family responsibilities, etc? If so, how can one make each of these elements more precise and combine them to form an overall view of priority – i.e. one patient's 'need' relative to another's?

At a more aggregate level, suppose you are a departmental official in the DHSS who has been instructed by the top of the office to investigate the extent to which the area distribution of community health and hospital resources in the NHS matches up with regional needs. Presumably, a large part of 'need', if not all of it, will relate to the prevalence or incidence of ill health in an area so you will naturally turn to the statistics, and there you will find on a regional basis sets of data relating to provision, expenditure, real inputs, patient throughputs, some limited data on consultation rates – but precious little on ill health. True, there are mortality data and life expectancy data, but we know that much sickness – and some of it serious, too – never gets recorded in morbidity statistics (such as GP consultation rates), and that many related statistics (such as sickness absence from work) are very poor proxies for ill health.

Finally, you may simply be fed up with being told about Britain's poor economic performance, and further depressed by the news that the UK fell from second place in the international league of infant mortality in 1960 (22.5 deaths per 1,000 live births) to fifth in 1972 (17.6 deaths per 1,000 live births) and want something a little more sophisticated in the way of international comparison of the quality of life (and one that may – but only 'may' – give the UK a boost in the chart ratings).

These illustrations point up the variety of purposes for which health status measures may be used. Thus, the following is a – probably not exhaustive – summary list of potential uses:

(i) for research purposes, e.g. in assessing the relative therapeutic advantages of alternative clinical procedures;

(ii)  in clinical practice, e.g. to monitor patient states, identify what is a 'sick' person, identify a 'recovery';

(iii)  in clinical rationing, e.g. to select patients by degree of priority;

(iv)  in health service planning, e.g. to identify consequences of policy decisions regarding, say, reducing length of in-patient stay, or to monitor the performance of the system in any number of respects;

(v)  in international comparisons.

If the health status measure is to do *any* of these jobs properly it should have a number of basic characteristics:

(i)  it should be reliable and reproduceable by different persons;

(ii)  it should be valid in the sense that it should measure what it purports to measure;

(iii)  it should be capable of being related to some of the variables over which the researcher, practitioner, administrator etc. has some control.

But it is also clear that the actual *form* of the measure would vary according to its purpose. For some purposes a very fine measure of specific attributes will be required; for others, relatively cruder measures will be sufficient, say, to plot the trends that are the principal object of interest. Thus, for example, crude mortality rates (per 1,000 population) are the standard measure, or indicator, of health in broad cross-country comparisons including both rich and poor countries. These are often supplemented by infant mortality rates (deaths of those aged under one year per 1,000 live births), which considerably complicates the picture, as the plot in figure 4.1 for the most recently available data shows, suggesting the interesting question: is the Isle of Man, with a high crude death rate and a low infant mortality rate, better or worse off than Norfolk Island, with a low crude death rate and high infant mortality? How to interpret the significance of the dimensions taken separately is one problem: the more infant lives that are saved, the greater the prevalence of handicap; the longer one may expect to live, the more geriatric problems one is likely to suffer. Clearly, as soon as one has more than one dimension in one's measure of the comparative health status of different national populations, and one country is not better off than the other on *both* dimensions, interpretation becomes even more difficult.

A more sophisticated comparison than the one just made would allow for the fact that the age and sex composition of populations may

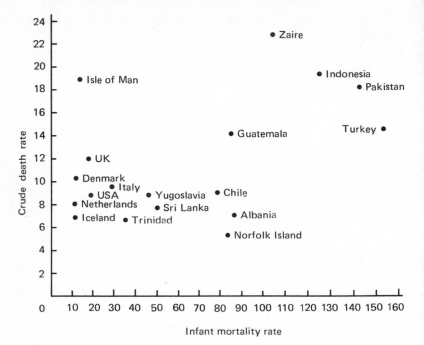

FIGURE 4.1 *Mortality and infant mortality rates in selected countries, 1972 (or latest available data)*

differ, and thus the crude death rate would be expected to differ without a higher one necessarily being validly interpreted as worse. In figure 4.2 the scatter is of 1973 infant mortality against mortality adjusted for age and sex and, for this relatively small area of the UK, for the fact that the density of certain types of hospital in an area can affect its mortality rate giving an unfair (i.e. invalid) idea of the relative basic healthiness of the various sub-areas. Once again, however, we see that the two indicators do not move together invariably, even after the adjustment has been made.

The principal value of broad indicators such as these is to indicate broad areas of — from the policy viewpoint — need. More specific policy formation in the health service as well as in other areas would, of course, require more detailed breakdowns of the data — for example, into cause of death — and supplementation with other mortality data such as neonatal mortality (deaths of infants under 4 months of age) and perinatal mortality (still-births and deaths under one week of age),

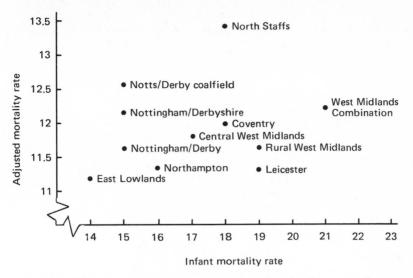

FIGURE 4.2 *Adjusted mortality and infant mortality in the East and West Midland standard regions, 1973*

as well as further supplementation by morbidity data such as GP visits, out-patient visits, sickness absence from work (all of which depend upon the individual's visiting a doctor or hospital) and the new General Household Survey sample data on limiting longstanding illness and short-term restriction of activity owing to acute sickness. These morbidity data are of crucial importance since it does not necessarily follow, of course, that a longer-lived population, or one in which fewer infants die, is also well and active.

For many purposes, however, such data simply will not do. Perhaps we are interested in following the health status of a particular and identifiable group of individuals through time – but published data do not enable this. Plainly, our neurosurgeon, our local welfare officer and our hospital consultant of the earlier examples would not find these data at all valuable because they would, in addition to being cross-sectional rather than longitudinal, be far too crude. For their purposes a different set of patient characteristics would be needed. For example, a list of the various dimensions along which elderly persons' ability to function has been measured in a ten-study survey by Wright (1974) is given in table 4.1. Each function might be classified by being awarded points on a scale: 0 = no difficulty, 1 = some difficulty,

TABLE 4.1.

*Components used in constructing an index of disability in ten studies of the elderly*

| Function | Frequency of use in the ten studies |
|---|---|
| Get into/or out of bed | 7 |
| Get into/or out of chair | 4 |
| Walk outdoors | 7 |
| Walk indoors | 8 |
| Move from wheelchair to bed | 1 |
| Propel wheelchair | 1 |
| Negotiate stairs | 8 |
| Wash hands and face | 8 |
| Comb hair (women only) | 2 |
| Shave (men only) | 2 |
| Bath or all-over wash | 7 |
| Dress | 9 |
| Fasten buttons and zips | 1 |
| Put on shoes and stockings | 1 |
| Use WC | 5 |
| Feed | 6 |
| Laundry | 1 |
| Cut toenails | 2 |
| Contenence | 6 |
| Prepare meals | 4 |
| Make a hot drink | 1 |
| Shop | 1 |
| Clean floors | 4 |

2 = great problems. In chapter 8 we shall be examining in closer detail the analogous problem for the consultant who cares to manage his hospital waiting list in an efficient and fair manner.

Whatever the purpose of the exercise, there are six quite crucial phases to the collection and evaluation of such measures or indicators of health (or ill health), of which the first three are:

(i) the choice of the dimensions of measurement (e.g. crude mortality rates, neonatal mortality rates, ability to cut toenails). These should plainly relate to the objective of the exercise and should be sufficiently complete. In a policy context, their selection amounts to a statement of a fairly precise kind about the dimensions in which it is proper to evaluate policy or, in other words, a statement about what health policy is about in a specified area. Inescapably, therefore, this phase involves someone making value judgements: the phase cannot be a purely scientific one;

(ii) a set of descriptive statements by which more or less of the attribute being measured can be identified. With mortality data this is straightforward. With other kinds of measure, however, such as 'psychological disturbance', the units of measurement may be harder to identify. This phase requires judgements, if the 'units' are to be useful ones, but it does not require the making of value judgements. There is no question, for example, that this phase is the proper province of the appropriate health professional;

(iii) the relative valuation of the units as identified and measured in (i) and (ii). While some of the ways in which this has been done are extremely crude and fail to perceive that at this stage some quite crucial value judgements are involved *that amount almost to a policy definition of need*, others have appreciated this crucial aspect of phase (iii) and have boldly faced up to the desirability of explicitly deciding *which are the more important degrees of, say, impairment and how much more severe are they.*

For example, the scale used to measure handicap in Amelia Harris's well-known study of handicap (Harris *et al.*, 1971) included ten dimensions, of which two, together with the units of measurement (descriptive categories) and the index scores of handicap, are shown in table 4.2.

The implications of such an approach can be brought out more clearly if we construct a matrix as in figure 4.3. There it can be seen that individuals fall into eight categories, with those who are least impaired receiving the score 0 and those most severely impaired receiving a score of 9. Whether we wish to interpret these numbers as *cardinal* measures, such that 4 is twice as bad as 2 and 9 three times as

TABLE 4.2.
*Illustrative dimensions from the Harris scale*

| Unit | 1 | 2<br>Some<br>difficulty<br>but can do | 3<br>Not<br>on | 4<br>Never<br>because<br>too |
|---|---|---|---|---|
| Dimension | No<br>difficulty | on own | own | difficult |
| Getting to or<br>using WC | 0 | 4 | 6 | 6 |
| Getting in and<br>out of bed | 0 | 2 | 3 | 3 |

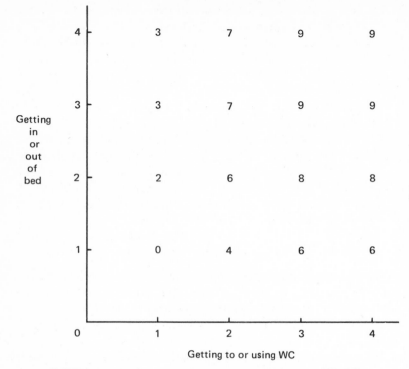

FIGURE 4.3 *Getting to or using WC: matrix of degrees of disability*

bad as 3, rather than as *ordinal* measures, such that 9 is worse than 8 is worse than 7 etc., without saying *how much worse*, will depend upon the purposes for which the exercise is to be used. Note, however, that value judgements have been utilised to make the 'trade-off' between different combinations of measures: thus the combination (2,2) is equally bad as the combination (1,4), each receiving a score of 6. One startling but inescapable interpretation of this is that if a course of treatment was applied to a patient whose current disability state was (2,2), with the effect of removing all problems in getting to bed but making it quite impossible for the person in question to use the WC (while no other effects on functioning occurred of any kind), the value judgement implicit in the Harris scale is that there would have been no net benefit at all — the procedure would have been, in a strictly relevant sense, useless.

While a great improvement on many other studies, this illustration points up some limitations of the procedure. First, as it stands, the scores corresponding to measures along the axes of the matrix are simply *additive*: the combination of two scores is simply their sum; no allowance is made for the clear possibility that one may wish to regard a combination of disability as *worse* than the sum of each considered separately. Second, its presentation as a matrix brings out the fact that there are not the differences that one might expect between all the combinations of disability. For some purposes, it may be sufficient to think of *areas* within the space of figure 4.3 rather than of points, for example, to take the 8s and 9s as one group, the 6s and 7s as another, the 3s and 4s as another and the 0s and 2s as yet another. This was essentially the categorisation procedure adopted in the Harris survey. For other purposes, however, still finer degrees of gradation are called for. In order to see what is really involved in this process it is useful to make it more abstract, so that both its logic and its generality become clearer. For every problem of health status measurement it will not be necessary to go into this detail, yet for some problems it will be and for *all* problems of measurement it is useful to know what the necessary logical steps are — as we shall see in moment, failure to perceive them can lead to quite serious oversight.

Figures 4.4 and 4.5 set out the basic steps and are reproduced from Culyer, Lavers and Williams (1971). As before, for expositional clarity we restrict ourselves to two dimensions (with three or more a mathematical rather than graphical representation would have to be used). $\alpha, \beta, \gamma, \delta$ are descriptive statements in one dimension and a,b,c,d,e are descriptive statements in the second dimension. Each symbol O,X,□ and △ refer to one of four specified patients (with different diseases, say, or disability problems) or to populations (with different social, economic or health environments). Each O in figure 4.4 represents a different expert's assessment of the condition. Thus we have three experts all assigning □-type patients or populations to the same point, as would be expected if the dimensions were fairly well identified and objective (such as measured mortality data). We also, however, have six experts assigning X-type patients or populations in a rather dispersed way. Such is likely to be the case with rather subjective statements about populations or patients and can arise where the dimensions correspond to outsiders' judgement about rather vaguely defined categories such as 'happiness', or where the medical condition, or population in question, or the descriptive statements themselves are not properly specified.

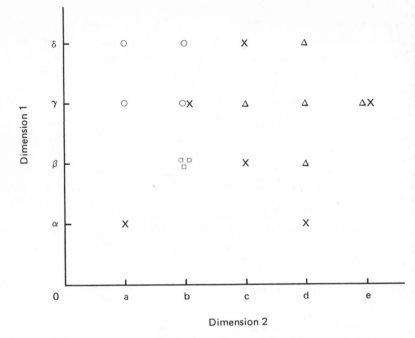

FIGURE 4.4 *Illustrative assignment of health states*

Fortunately, empirical studies, even in subjective-sounding areas like pain measurement (see, e.g., Rosser and Watts, 1972), indicate that problems of disagreement among expert assessors can be overcome, provided that too many categories in each dimension are avoided and that all relevant aspects of the assignment problem are clearly and unambiguously defined.

The next stage involves the essence of phase (iii), where we now explicitly establish the trade-off between each cell in the agreed matrix — for example, is combination γa better or worse than combination βc? This pairwise comparison can now be seen very clearly to involve a value judgement, but one that tends to be hidden in other, less formal, ways of interpreting the assessments. Figure 4.5 shows the pattern that may be revealed after all the relevant pairwise comparisons have been made. The contour lines connect all states that are regarded as equally bad: for example, (γ,O), (β,a), (α,b) and (O,d) are, in this example, equally bad. If the dimensions describe increasing severity of ill health as one moves out from the origin along the axes, then all

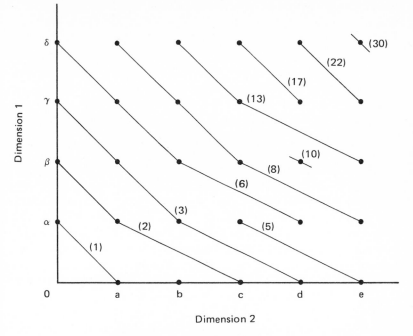

FIGURE 4.5  *Trade-offs of health states*

contour lines above the one joining γ and d are 'worse' and all those lower are 'better'. In this way, all states of health have been ranked one against the other, with those regarded as equivalent identified as well.

The fourth phase in evaluating health status can most conveniently be explained using figure 4.5, and it is to assign numbers to the contours indicating the relative severity of one contour to another. It is this phase that produces the final indicator or measure of health status. In the figure, the numbers in brackets represent such an assignment, where state (6) is evaluated as twice as bad as state (3), etc. The interpretation is similar to that in the Harris matrix of figure 4.3 save that we have not arrived at the final scoring by the rather naive procedure of *adding* separate scores on the dimensions, but have explicitly attached relative valuations to *combinations* for, as is frequently the case, the whole can easily be more than the mere sum of its parts. Moreover, we no longer have equivalence between points that are unambiguously better or worse than others on each dimension. The numbers are, of course, illustrative. It may well be that the *difference* between each contour score would increase (1,2,4,7, etc.) rather than remain constant (1,2,3,4, etc.) or vary as in figure 4.5. This will depend upon the value judgements made in each case. Note also that the value judgement required in phase (iii) (establishing equivalence) is not the same as that here in phase (iv), which establishes the cardinal ranking between contours and which yields the health status indicator itself.

Phase (v) is necessary if at any time the estimated improvement in the health index is to be used in justification of resource use. This phase involves relating the alternative procedures proposed to the expected outcome, in terms of improved health, in order that an intelligent choice can be made about the least-cost method of attaining any chosen improvement. Straightforward though it may seem, this is an area where substantial ignorance often prevails even about the crude outcomes of alternative procedures. Partly, the reason for this lies in the absence, hitherto, of any detailed methodology for measuring health status in epidemiological and medical research; partly in medical ethics, which may preclude the necessary experimentation to discover effective treatments or the relative efficacy of different treatments; and partly in inertia. We shall, however, take up these issues in much greater detail in chapter 5.

The final phase of evaluation, phase (vi), occurs only when it is necessary to compare the value of the outcome, in terms of improvement in health status, with the cost of the inputs used to effect it. It is clearly crucial in 'grand' questions concerning, say, the 'ideal' size of the NHS *vis-à-vis* other public sector departments, and it occasionally is necessary within the NHS if, for example, one wishes to work out its social 'profitability' or, more modestly, the social 'profitability' of a particular bit of it. More frequently it may become necessary when one is comparing various procedures having clearly different costs but also different outcomes in terms of health improvements. In such cases, when the socially costlier technique also produces a larger gain in health status, the choice of technique clearly will depend upon the social value placed on the differential gain in health status, or reduction in need, relative to the cost differential. Once again, however, this leads us directly into questions concerning the efficiency of health care supply and is more properly the subject of the next chapter.

Two principal points of substantial *general* importance emerge from our discussion. First, although we have spelled out rather formally the necessary phases in measuring health (or ill health), it is the case that less formal methods inescapably — as a matter of logic — also require each phase to be gone through though it may be done only implicitly. Of course, for many purposes the detailed procedures we have identified are not necessary, but in other cases each will be necessary and in every case it is useful to be aware of what one is inescapably doing, whether one is being implicit or explicit about it. At the end of this chapter some dangers inherent in the implicit approach where one is also not aware of the implications of one's procedures are illustrated from a recently published proposal in a medical journal.

The second general point is that our procedure underlines the fact that analysis identifies the necessary value judgements that have to be made in measuring health. It is not and cannot be a purely scientific endeavour. The value judgements that must inevitably be made concern:

(i)  choice of dimensions in which health state is to be basically measured (phase (i));
(ii) the relative valuation of combinations of characteristics in the dimensions above measured (phase (iii));
(iii) the absolute valuation of the combinations (phase (iv));
(iv) the translation of the absolute valuations of health into a valuation relative to the value of the resources to be used (phase (vi)).

It is a question of major importance as to who should be making these value judgements in the NHS. At present, it is generally the case that health professionals, explicitly or implicitly, make each and every one of them. Yet now that we have identified them rather carefully, it seems far from clear that this is consistent with the objectives of the NHS. One set of categories of appropriate persons that seems less inappropriate is the following:

(i)  ultimate clients (i.e. patients, populations), with help from experts whose role it would be to make suggestions, eliminate redundant dimensions, refine the dimensions and keep them relevant to the purpose for which the exercise is designed;
(ii) patients in principle, again with help from professionals. In many cases, professionals, especially doctors, will have to act for patients or it will be more convenient for them to do so. At all times however the agent should act as an agent, not as an imposer of his own values. This is, perhaps, the core of the ideal doctor—patient relationship;

(iii) this value judgement must normally be made by medical practitioners or social workers in a clinical situation (e.g. in selecting the most urgent cases). However there is much to be said, in a *national* health service, for some consistency of practice and, hence, for some general framework of values within which to operate. At another level, that of planning resource deployments, the value judgements are appropriately made by those with public accountability for such decisions, e.g. area health authorities or the central authorities;

(iv) this value judgement is also, essentially, a planning matter about policy in the NHS and is again appropriately taken by publicly accountable planners.

In practice, of course, all will interact and mutually inform one another. Equally, however, it is clear that the idea of the NHS is not consistent with a random hit-and-miss approach. The making of value judgements lies at the heart of medical care delivery in general, is crucial in the concept of the NHS and is the very essence of establishing the meaning of the word 'need'.

While there exists a number of studies designed for specific purposes (some are listed in the bibliography, while still others are referred to in these references) and which vary in quality and perception of the issues, the major gaping hole is in the lack of systematic information about morbidity in the UK with the NHS. As has been mentioned, mortality data are too crude for most purposes, other than the most general, within a country while existing morbidity data are subject to serious interpretational problems. The advantage of the General Household Survey is that it has a comprehensive coverage and is quite detailed. It is, however, not yet possible to relate its findings to much other published data on population and population characteristics. Of longitudinal studies, following through the health experience of a specified set of individuals or 'clients', we are currently deprived, however. So the real 'crunch' question of making sure that the NHS's resources go to those whose needs are greatest and can be most reduced remains, at present, unanswerable — we cannot, in general, monitor and we cannot, in general, assess. The work currently in progress at the University of York under Alan Williams (1974) and K. G. Wright (1974) is only the beginning of the assault on this most conspicuously absent of the informational needs of health service managers.

We conclude with the cautionary tale of how an imaginative

initiative that began with the best of intentions omitted to make explicit some of the crucial aspects of health status indexes we have mentioned above. Hence it camouflaged many judgements (some of them value judgements) which, had they been made more explicit, might have led to a rather different kind of index than the one they derived.

The exercise was a proposal for measuring health put forward jointly by an anaesthetist and a doctor (Grogono and Woodgate, 1971). The exercise was prompted by the same kind of observation that prompts the present book: 'we have as yet no national basis upon which to organise and distribute our resources. This must in part be attributed to the absence of any method of measuring efficacy: we have no method of measuring a patient's health before and after treatment.' After consultation with patients and colleagues they settled on ten broad aspects of human functioning that were, taken together, comprehensive and were intended as the basis for making better statements about patient states than what they described as the customary 'fit for light duty only' or 'better than yesterday', etc.

The ten dimensions were as set out in table 4.3. A score was to be assigned according to the scale indicated and in each of the dimensions. The scores were then totalled. By implication, each of the ten factors has an equal weight (for failure to ascribe *any* weights is equivalent here to assuming *equal* weights) and the degree of seriousness of malfunction is both linear and simply additive (a person with five 1s for the first five

TABLE 4.3.
*Components of the Grogono-Woodgate index*

|  | normal (= 1) | impaired (= ½) | incapacitated (= 0) |
|---|---|---|---|
| 1. Ability to work | | | |
| 2. Hobbies and recreation | | | |
| 3. Malaise, pain or suffering | | | |
| 4. Worry or unhappiness | | | |
| 5. Ability to communicate | | | |
| 6. Ability to sleep | | | |
| 7. Independence of others | | | |
| 8. Ability to eat/enjoy food | | | |
| 9. Bladder and bowels | | | |
| 10. Sex life | | | |
| Total | | | |

dimensions and five 0s for the second five is judged just as bad as a person having the 1s and the 0s reversed, or one scoring ½ on each of the ten).

They found the index to be workable with a high degree of consensus among those assigning the points. But they did not identify the value judgements they were implicitly making and, despite the fact that 'there did not seem to be any anomalies', it seems somewhat unlikely that the priorities they were attaching implicitly were actually those that they would have chosen had the underlying logic of the procedure they were using been clear to them. Had more attention been paid to such matters, the weights may have ceased to be unitary and constant — indeed a much more adequate representation of the true humanity to which health status measurement should aspire would have been possible.

Not least among the interesting aspects of this experiment, however, is the evidence it supplies that the kind of concern focused on in this book is shared not merely by academics, administrators and planners. The desirability of an unambiguous measure of outcome (and hence of need) is seen also by clinical researchers and some clinical practitioners. If our steps are at times somewhat halting, there is little doubt about the direction in which we are going.

We have returned to the clinical situation. Let us end this chapter with some reflections from one of Britain's leading neurosurgeons:

Perhaps the most serious of all mis-directions of effort is the vigorous and sometimes prolonged treatment of patients with brain damage so extensive that, although death may be deferred, the postponement brings to the family and to society only misery and expense. This is *unsuccessful* treatment. While some such patients recover to varying degrees, others are left as a human shell, awake but vacant, speechless and spastic and with no evidence of a functioning mind either receiving or projecting information, a testimony to the triumph of technology over humanity . . . [T] he wooly terms used by neurosurgeons to describe recovery ('worthwhile', 'useful', 'practical', . . . [are] . . . a serious hindrance when it comes to comparing the efficacy of different regimes of management and to stabilising prognostic criteria. [Jennett, 1974]

And what is dramatic, soul-rending but crucial in neurosurgery is all-pervasive, if less dramatic and mercifully often less soul-rending, throughout the health services.

Do we really have to think in the way suggested in this chapter? Could we not, at least for most 'social' purposes, perform *ad hoc* social surveys of life-styles, economic and social characteristics, with mortality and morbidity data of the conventional sort thrown in? The answer must be 'no', because, although the data thus collected may be appropriate for some purposes, their interpretation either as indicators of outcome or, more powerfully, as indicators of need requires *inescapably* that each of the steps we have described be taken. In so far as the more conventional sorts of 'appraisal' are 'comfortable', they are comfortable precisely because, in the welter of description and subjective judgement upon which they characteristically rely, they pretend that the issues we have discussed do not need to be resolved. But the NHS requires above all that both straight analysis and the apparent facts and value judgements be discussed and argued about, and for that they must not only be brought right out into the open but honed down to a level of precision that enables us to know *precisely* what it is that is being discussed and *precisely* what it is (if anything) that has been missed out but which may be relevant. Only then will the language of need get the press it deserves and not the press it has often − and not undeservedly − got. The criterion for judging the argument of this chapter, therefore, is not whether the dimensions etc. of the measures discussed are the 'right' ones, but whether the method of deciding such things that has been proposed is as exhaustively comprehensive in including every potentially relevant factor as it is claimed to be.

If the answer to that question is 'yes', then we can proceed immediately to the empirical part of the first stage of evaluating need.

## BIBLIOGRAPHY

Acheson, E. D. (1968) 'Some remarks on contemporary British Medical Statistics' *Journal of the Royal Statistical Society*, A, vol. 131

Bauer, R. A. (ed) (1966) *Social Indicators* Cambridge, MIT Press

Berg, R. L. (ed) (1973) *Health Status Indexes* Chicago, Hospital Research and Educational Trust

Butterfield, W. J. H. (1968) *Priorities in Medicine* London, Nuffield Provincial Hospitals Trust

Card, W. I. (1973) 'Computer-Assisted Diagnosis and Pattern Recognition: the computing approach to clinical diagnosis' *Proceedings of the Royal Society London*, vol. 184

Culyer, A. J. (1972) 'Indicators of health: an economist's viewpoint' in Laing (1972)

Culyer, A. J. (1972) 'Appraising Government Expenditure on Health Services: the problems of "need" and "output" ' *Public Finance,* vol. 27

Culyer, A. J. (ed.) (1974) *Economic Policies and Social Goals: Aspects of Public Choice* London, Martin Robertson

Culyer, A. J., Lavers, R. J. and Williams, Alan (1971) 'Social indicators: Health' *Social Trends*, no. 2

Department of Health and Social Security (various), *Health and Personal Social Services Statistics* London, HMSO

Doll, R. (1974) 'Surveillance and Monitoring' *International Journal of Epidemiology*, vol. 2

Fanshel, S. (1972) 'A Meaningful Measure of Health for Epidemiology' *International Journal of Epidemiology*, vol. 1.

Fanshel, S. and Bush, J. W. (1970) 'A Health Status Index and its Application to Health Services Outcomes' *Operations Research*, vol. 18

Friedsam, H. J. and Martin, H. W. (1963) 'A Comparison of Self and Physicians' Health Ratings in an Older Population' *Journal of Health and Human Behaviour*, vol. 4

Garrard, J. and Bennett, A. E. (1971) 'A validated interview schedule for use in population surveys of chronic disease and disability' *British Journal of Preventive and Social Medicine*, vol. 25

Grogono, A. W. and Woodgate, D. J. (1971) 'Index for Measuring Health' *The Lancet* 6 November

Hamilton, M. (1960) 'A rating scale for depression' *Journal of Neurological Psychiatry* vol. 23

Harris, A. *et al.* (1971) *Handicapped and Impaired in Great Britain* London, HMSO

Jennett, B. (1974) 'Surgeon of the Seventies' *Journal of the Royal College of Surgeons of Edinburgh*, vol. 19

Laing, W. A. (1972) *Evaluation in the Health Services* London, Office of Health Economics

Office of Population Censuses and Surveys (1973) *The General Household Survey* London, HMSO

Rosser, R. and Watts, V. (1972) 'The Measurement of Hospital Output' *International Journal of Epidemiology*, vol. 1

Patrick, D. L., Bush, J. W. and Chen, M. M. (1973) 'Methods for Measuring Levels of Well-being for a Health Status Index' *Health Services Research* vol. 8

Sellin, T. and Wolfgang, M. E. (1964) *The Measurement of Delinquency* New York, Wiley

Shonfield, A. and Shaw, S. (1972) *Social Indicators and Social Policy* London, Heinemann

Sullivan, D. (1966) *Conceptual problems in developing an index of health* Washington DC, Department of Health, Education and Welfare

Wager, R. (1972) *The Care of the Elderly* London, CIPFA

Williams, Alan (1974) 'Measuring the effectiveness of health care systems' *British Journal of Preventive and Social Medicine* vol. 28

Wright, K. G. (1974) 'Alternative measures of the output of social programmes: the elderly' in Culyer (1974)

Zyzanski, S. J., Hulka, B. and Cassell, J. C. (1974) 'Scale for Measurement of "Satisfaction" with Medical Care: modifications in content, format and scoring' *Medical Care*, vol. 12

# 5.   Medical Technology, Effectiveness and Efficiency : History and Concepts

In this and the next chapter we survey the context of medical care in promoting better health and discuss ways in which economic analysis can complement epidemiological work in planning an efficient service. Since much of the literature overlaps, the bibliography for both chapters is appended to chapter 6.

For the greater part of man's history, the relatively crude information provided by population and mortality data is sufficient to chart the story of the social impact of medicine. The remarkable fact appears to be that only after the twentieth century was well into its majority was it possible to produce any evidence that the clinical procedures of medicine had any substantial impact on health.

Causes of death were first registered in Britain in 1838, and there is little doubt that the principal factor contributing to population increase since (and probably before) that time was a decline in mortality rates owing to a reduction in the number of deaths from communicable diseases. Since mortality was falling and life expectancy was rising before the causes of death were properly understood, the reduction cannot be attributed to medical science. Knowledge of smallpox was an exception to the relative ignorance prevailing in the eighteenth and nineteenth centuries, and inoculation against smallpox in the eighteenth century has been held by economic historians to be the principal explanation for the dramatic population rise after 1700. Although the increase was relatively small from 1700 to 1750, after the middle of the eighteenth century population rose rapidly and steadily right through to end of the nineteenth century. From 1750 to 1850 the best estimates indicate that population increased threefold.

Despite the plausibility of this thesis, it has been asserted that the crude process of inoculation with infected material, even had it been done with the most effective of modern vaccines, cannot really have had such an impact. On the other hand, there is no doubt that better nutrition can enable people the better to withstand viruses — especially with tuberculosis, rickets and other chronic diseases accounting for a large proportion of all deaths. Unfortunately, there is some doubt that nutrition improved markedly at this time, partly because population rose at least as fast as agricultural productivity. Personal hygiene, however, did improve quite substantially after 1800, and this would account especially for the reduction of incidence of diseases of the intestinal tract (e.g. gastroenteritis, typhoid fever and dysentery) and diseases transmitted by body lice (e.g. typhus, relapsing fever and trench fever). The sanitary reforms of the nineteenth century also had an undisputed impact on mortality. Adequate drainage, refuse disposal away from publicly frequented places and the improvement of water supplies began to be introduced generally halfway through the nineteenth century; the decline in mortality from intestinal infections such as cholera is alone an adequate indicator of their effectiveness.

Until the twentieth century, then, it would appear that, apart from any spontaneous declines in the virulence of disease that may have occurred (and such phenomena do appear to have had substantial impact) and the probable impact of inoculation on smallpox mortality, the chief agents improving the health of the British people were improved personal hygiene and sanitary measures. The activities of the medics, whether the humble apothecary or the fellows of the hugely prestigious Royal College of Physicians, were relatively insignificant (McKeown and Record, 1962; Razzell, 1965, 1974; McKeown, 1971; McKeown et al., 1972).

During the twentieth century, entirely new developments in medical technology and, especially, in pharmacology made it possible for the first time for medical intervention to have a broad and indisputable impact on the natural history of many diseases, especially infectious diseases. The principal causes of death today are cancers, heart disease, cerebrovascular disease, pneumonia and bronchitis, all of which strike older persons (see table 5.1). Mortality rarely occurs before the age of

TABLE 5.1.
*Percentage of deaths by cause, 1972*

| | |
|---|---|
| Tuberculosis | 0.26 |
| Venereal disease | 0.02 |
| Cancer of: | |
| digestive system | 6.67 |
| lung, bronchus, trachea | 5.36 |
| breast | 1.89 |
| cervix | 0.37 |
| Leukemia | 0.52 |
| Diabetes | 0.92 |
| Cerebrovascular disease | 14.06 |
| Chronic rheumatic heart disease | 1.11 |
| Hypertensive heart disease | 1.52 |
| Ischaemic heart disease | 25.98 |
| Influenza | 0.52 |
| Pneumonia (except newborn) | 7.38 |
| Bronchitis | 4.88 |
| Motor vehicle accidents | 1.19 |
| All other accidents | 1.88 |
| Suicide and self inflicted injury* | 0.64 |
| Other causes | 24.83 |

*Almost certainly substantially under-reported.
*Source: Social Trends* London, HMSO (1974), table 94.

forty-five and is even then unlikely to be caused by infection or contagion from another diseased person, but rather by a road accident. There has also been a remarkable reduction in the severity of spells of morbidity. Effective treatments now exist for pernicious anaemia, high blood pressure, juvenile diabetes, rheumatic disease, allergies and respiratory diseases and mental illness. Simple surgical repair work on hernias, haemorrhoids, prolapsed wombs etc. is now a matter of routine with only minor risks attached. The wonders of modern surgery have become effectively applicable only in the last two decades with the development of anaesthesiology, which has made long and complicated operations on the vital organs both safer for the patient and easier for the surgeon.

The great killers of previous centuries — the infectious diseases — are, with the possible exception of influenza, almost entirely vanquished. The great decline in mortality from pneumonia began only, however, in the 1940s, as did death rates from diphtheria and tuberculosis. Today, the diseases from which men die in Britain are chronic and their onset insidious. The major impact of the pharmaceutical revolution on bacterial infections and spirochaetal diseases such as syphilis (stemming mainly from the antibiotics) and on virus diseases (mainly preventative rather than curative) is for the most part probably over. Once again, the biggest contributors to further reductions in morbidity are most likely to be environmental. But while once it was an environment of proverty that killed, today it is an environment of wealth: traffic accidents, smoking, obesity and the emotional stress of urban living are among the principal causes of mortality and morbidity.

This, then, appears to have been the broad pattern. Until the 1930s the chief causes of improvements in health were improvements in the environment. From the 1930s to the 1950s the chief contributors to better health were drugs and new surgical techniques. In the 1960s the revolution in psychotropic drugs took place and effective treatment of mental illness became possible for the first time. The same period saw the introduction of really effective drugs against high blood pressure. Today, the major sources of further improvement appear once more to be environmental. The wheel has come full circle. (Though the drug industry is still, fortunately, introducing ever improved and finer psychopharmacological products – with fewer bad side effects and quicker action. The next decade is likely to see more effective treatment for schizophrenia, and the possibility still exists, of course, of effective chemotherapy for viral infections and chemotherapy with immunotherapy for cancer.)

Diagnosis (the identification of a condition) and treatment are today highly technical procedures. But the mystique and prestige of medical science (so different from its status in the nineteenth century and before) can serve to give a false picture of its precision. Now it is increasingly difficult to distinguish unambiguously between a healthy and a diseased state using technological measurements. In diagnosis, for example, a characteristic problem is the overlapping distributions of a symptom for healthy and sick persons. For many measurable symptoms, especially haematological and biochemical ones, the distribution curves appear as in figure 5.1.

For haemoglobin levels, blood pressure, blood sugar levels and several other testable indicators, a decision has to be taken as to how far above or below average a measure must read before action is warranted. Observer error exists. A 1966 study found, in a study of the differences between eight radiologists' ability to detect Paterson–Kelly webs in X-ray photographs of the barium swallow of 132 patients

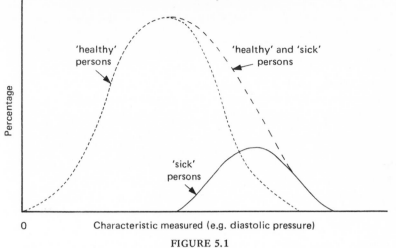

'healthy'
persons

'healthy' and 'sick'
persons

Percentage

'sick'
persons

0            Characteristic measured (e.g. diastolic pressure)

FIGURE 5.1

*Source:* based on charts in A. L. Cochrane (1972) p. 40.

having dysphagia (difficulty with swallowing) that the number of subjects in whom a web was detected varied from 6 to 59 per cent (these 'webs' in the throat show up as a kind of pouch in X-rays of patients who have taken a barium swallow) (Elwood and Pitman, 1966). Blood pressure readings are subject to similar errors. Even among the most experienced hospital doctors, diagnoses can vary quite markedly. Table 5.2 compares the diagnoses made by consultants in a major hospital with the final diagnosis reached, usually after surgery had taken place. For one common condition, appendicitis, only 75 of the 85 cases were correctly diagnosed by the most experienced men in the hospital. Not surprisingly, the success rate of less senior doctors was substantially lower.

Appropriate treatment is likewise far from being as easy and unambiguous to identify as may be popularly thought. There is generally a choice of treatment. In an appendix to the Sainsbury Committee's report on the pharmaceutical industry, 455 general practitioners prescribed over 30 different prescriptions for each of five common illnesses. Only 8 out of a total of 2,275 prescriptions were found to be unacceptably toxic or ineffectual, but the cost variation was substantial. For painful osteo-arthritis, for example, 11 per cent of GPs recommended Indocid at a prescription cost of 180*d* while 10 per cent recommended aspirin at a cost of 2*d*.

TABLE 5.2.

*Diagnoses made by senior clinicians in charge of case: 304 patients with acute abdominal pain (Leeds 1971).*

| Senior clinical diagnosis | 1 | 2 | 3 | 4 | 5 | 6 | 7 | 8 | Total |
|---|---|---|---|---|---|---|---|---|---|
| Final diagnosis | | | | | | | | | |
| 1 Appendicitis | 75 | 1 | 6 | — | — | — | — | 3 | 85 |
| 2 Diverticular disease | — | 2 | — | 1 | — | — | — | 1 | 4 |
| 3 Perforated duodenal ulcer | 1 | — | 5 | — | — | — | — | 1 | 7 |
| 4 Non specific pain | 27 | — | 1 | 117 | 2 | — | 1 | 1 | 149 |
| 5 Cholecystitis | — | — | — | — | 20 | 1 | 3 | 2 | 26 |
| 6 Small bowel obstruction | — | — | — | — | — | 17 | — | — | 17 |
| 7 Pancreatitis | — | 1 | 1 | — | 1 | — | 5 | — | 8 |
| 8 Other | 3 | 1 | — | 1 | — | 1 | — | 2 | 8 |
| Total | 106 | 5 | 13 | 119 | 23 | 19 | 9 | 10 | 304 |

*Source:* F. T. de Dombal *et al.* (1972).

Although there may be choice of treatment in treating illness, not all treatments are equally effective. There is substantial evidence from randomised controlled trials that high blood pressure reduces expectation of life and consequently the diagnosis 'low blood pressure' has fallen into disuse in Britain — though not in Japan and most other European countries. Hospital practices can also vary widely. For example, despite strong evidence that bed rest is unimportant in the treatment of pulmonary tuberculosis, the mean length of stay in hospital is falling only slowly and is very variable from specialist to specialist (in one recent survey nearly 20 per cent of male patients were discharged in under a month and all within three months; in another, 10 per cent were discharged in under a month and over 20 per cent were still in hospital after a year).

Hospitalisation is, of course, extremely costly. Some costly treatments in hospital may actually do patients harm. There is evidence that surgery for small-celled cancer of the bronchus reduces life expectancy compared with radiography without surgery. Intensive care in hospital coronary care units has the effect, it appears, of reducing life expectancy for coronary patients compared with bed rest at home. When death approaches a relatively young patient, dramatic and costly interventions may be undertaken, of little or no therapeutic value in terms of improving the prognosis, whose major value seems to be to provide evidence that 'all possible is being done'.

The effects of several standard treatments on the natural history of disease is unknown or in dispute. Tonsillectomy, for example, is the commonest cause for the admission of children to hospital, but the operation has a positive (if small) fatality rate and so should not be undertaken lightly. Yet there is evidence to suggest that the best medical treatment for the condition may be superior, or not inferior, to surgery. Certainly, admissions for tonsillectomy vary enormously per head of population from region to region in Britain (from 234 per 100,000 population in Sheffield to 410 in Oxford in 1971). The treatment of mature diabetes is in doubt, as compared with diabetes in the young, for whom insulin appears effective. Modern psychiatry is replete with therapies whose theoretical foundations are in dispute and whose effectiveness remains very largely untested in any systematic way.

Finally, modern therapies have introduced new considerations into the choice of technique: detection of abnormalities in foetuses still in the womb raises the question of abortion as a probably increasingly common surgical operation done on clinical grounds; contraception; spare part surgery (including blood transfusion); euthanasia in an increasingly ageing population — all raise major ethical problems of choice for patients, doctors and society.

This preliminary excursion into medical technology from 1700 to today has not been inflicted on the reader with the intention of belittling the great achievements of medical science and the fine chemical industry or of pretending that we know more about epidemiology or medicine than epidemiologists and doctors. Rather, the intention has been to put the medical achievement in its historical context and to disabuse the reader of many commonly held fallacies about the nature of medical 'productive processes' by using some of the results of modern epidemiological and medical knowledge. Rarely does any person have an unambiguously identifiable 'need' for any *specific* course of medical action. Medical inputs are widely substitutable. Increased real spending on known clinical techniques alone is unlikely, these days, to have a substantial payoff in terms of improved health.

At the same time the NHS is very big business, employing nearly one million people and spending over £3,000m. a year of taxpayers' (patients' in another guise) money. For most of its services the patients pay nothing at all, or are heavily subsidised. Hospitals, which spend two-thirds of the total, seem to enjoy, even under the new organisation of NHS, substantial autonomy within the system of accountability to district management teams, to area health authorities, to regional health authorities and, ultimately, to the Department of Health and Social Security. Devolution of decision-making has always been a feature of the NHS since its inception in 1948, and, within a hospital's budget, substantial discretion exists as regards methods of treatment, intensiveness of treatment (such as length of hospital in-patient stay), selection of patients (and length of waiting list, waiting time) and so on. It will not be our task here to investigate the effectiveness, in clinical terms, of various procedures — that is plainly the proper province of medical science. It will be clear, however, that the proper province of the economist — efficiency — depends upon the kind of technical information about procedures and their outcomes (see chapter 4) that medical science should, but frequently does not, provide. This is a problem with which we, like the managers of the NHS, will simply have to come to terms.

In the remainder of this chapter we shall illustrate the principal ways in which efficiency problems would be tackled in a rational NHS by examining studies that have been done and commenting both on their strong and their weak points. As a preliminary, however, let us review some of the common terminology that is associated with efficiency — terminology that suffers from the fact that it has both a loose and variable common usage and a much more precise economic meaning. It is, of course, in the direction of precision of meaning that we shall lean. (For a superb but introductory survey of ways of applying efficiency concepts in the social services generally, see the outstandingly articulate book by Williams and Anderson, 1975.)

The distinction between effectiveness and efficiency has already been alluded to in chapter 4's discussion of measuring health. From the point of view of efficiency, it cannot be emphasised too strongly that, even if doctors devotedly served their patients with all the clinical skills at their command, using the most up-to-date technology, equipment and buildings, intervening when there is the remotest chance of beneficially affecting a patient's condition, worthy though all this may sound, it is most unlikely they would be operating in an *efficient* fashion. This may readily be seen by considering that an effective intervention of the type described may (i) represent only a small improvement in actual outcome and patient comfort relative to the alternatives that exist; (ii) involve only a small social value of whatever improvement is effected; and (iii) involve additional costs that are higher than the social value of the improved outcomes. Of course, none of these things is necessarily true, but consideration of them does lead us to think about what considerations we would take into account in deciding whether or not a procedure was efficient.

First, any socially efficient procedure must, indeed, be *effective* in a clinical or engineering sense. That is to say, there should be some identifiable improvement (or a positive probability of such improvement) either immediately or subsequently in patient health states where these are defined sufficiently broadly to include the outcomes of purely caring as well as curing procedures. Secondly, any socially efficient procedure should be *technically efficient*. That is to say, any given procedure should not use up more resources than are strictly required by the technology employed. Typically there exists a variety of technologies using different combinations of resources such as hospital bed weeks, hospital manpower hours, out-patient resource hours, patient time, drugs, etc., etc. Each of these is technically efficient in producing a given outcome (which for conceptual purposes we may think of as an increase in a health index for a patient or set of patients) if it uses the minimum amount of resources regarded as necessary to achieve that outcome. Of these efficient techniques, the *cost-effective* technique is that which has the least cost out of the set that is relevant for the task in hand (clearly, it need not be the most spectacular, chrome-plated or modern technique). The cost-effective technique is not, however, necessarily socially efficient (though it is usual to expect it to be socially better than a cost-ineffective technique!), since it is always possible that we are doing something we should not be doing, even if we are doing it in a highly cost-effective way. More generally, cost effectiveness tells us nothing about either whether something should be done at all or, if it should be done, how much of it should be done. Since the cost usually varies with the amount being done (because, for example, of 'scale' economies) and the additional cost of doing more is rarely zero, the decision about the ideal amount to be doing cannot be made without considering cost, so full social efficiency can be defined only when the costs and the benefits are compared. If the difference between the full social costs and benefits is maximised, then – conceptually – we have full social efficiency. Normally, in a fully socially efficient programme we would expect there to be some residual unrealised benefit (unmet need) for the simple reason that the social value of realising that benefit would be less than the social cost of doing so and other things, then, would take priority.

The innocent-sounding adjective 'social' qualifying many of the nouns in the preceding paragraphs is crucial and must also be given precise meaning. 'Cost' is frequently identified with expenditures. As will be emphasised in chapter 6, however, there is no more reason to be obsessed with, say, hospital cash spending (save in that available cash defines the budget limits and helps public spending to be monitored and audited) than there is to be with consumer prices for health care. The first connotation of 'social' with respect to cost is, however, that even if we identify cost with expenditures our focus should not be solely on *hospital* expenditures when evaluating the efficiency of the hospital system. Hospital care usually implies some expenditure by the primary care sector (e.g. by GPs, by local authorities, by families). An expenditure-minimising hospital sector that thrust huge additional costs on other sectors (by, for example, too early discharges) clearly need not be efficient − technically or socially. Thus, *all* the costs (expenditures) should be taken account of.

The second major context of 'social' with regard to cost is that it invites us to look beyond the monetary 'veil'. Contrary to a mischievous popular view to the contrary, neither economics nor efficiency is particularly concerned with *money*. To the extent that it is concerned, it is because money prices, incomes and expenditures provide units of account, enabling unlike things to be compared in like terms. But not all costs carry money prices − family time or patient time is not paid for by the NHS but may have a real cost in that it could have been used for some other socially valued use, where the patient's own use for his time is a part of its social use (by definition we must surely count patients as members of society!). Similarly, existing capital assets, or crown property, or land already held freehold, tend to be treated as if they had zero cost because they carry no charges for further use, yet their use for one purpose denies their use for another, whose sacrifice is the cost. Usually, within organisations, resources are transferred without a price − because, of course, price systems are costly to operate − but we may wish to assign a 'shadow' price to that resource and act as though we actually had to pay it (e.g. the transfer of human blood from the Blood Transfusion Service to hospitals). Sometimes, resources may carry a price but one may have reason to suppose it is a poor reflection of the opportunity cost to society of using the resource in the NHS (e.g. low-grade labour that may otherwise be unemployed and hence has a very low or even zero alternative use value to society).

The context of 'social' on the benefit side is similar; namely, all benefits should be reckoned, to whomsoever they accrue and regardless of whether they carry a price. Pricing on the benefit side is, of course, almost entirely absent in the NHS precisely so that our notion of benefit is not distorted away from unpriced and humanitarian sources of benefit — in short, the reduction of need. While, however, removal of prices may have removed distortion, it also leaves us rather in the dark as to what the value of the benefits is. It is rather as if we have said that the bulb causes shadows so let us turn off the bulb!

Two other notions that are related to one another and require some explanation are those of 'discounting' and 'present value'. An important aspect of time in efficiency studies relates to the fact that costs and benefits can be dated — the cost and benefit consequences of decisions stretch forward into the future. Since the community prefers benefits sooner and likes to defer costs, future costs and benefits are *discounted* by an interest rate that in principle measures the rate at which the present and the future are substituted. Many philosophical and technical issues arise in the context of what the correct rate of discount should be so that all the discounted future costs and benefits can be added up to their *present value*. For practical purposes, there is much to be said for the common practice of using a variety of discounted rates (to test the sensitivity of the results) among which would be that rate which H.M. Treasury rules shall be used anyway in decision-making in the public sector.

Finally, 'shortage' is eternally cropping up. For our purposes, 'shortage' does not mean 'wouldn't it be nice to have more, say, doctors' or even 'we could practise better medicine if we had more doctors'. A 'shortage' exists quite simply when an efficient programme cannot be carried out for lack of some relevant resource. Thus, if it is economically efficient to carry out a particular programme, and we need more doctors to do it effectively, and we have not at the moment got them, then we have a shortage of doctors. (The familiar textbook definition of shortage as occurring when, at the going price, there is an excess demand for a resource, a service or a good is but a special case of this more general definition which requires, among other things, significance — for efficiency — to be attached to going prices.) Conversely, 'waste' exists when we are carrying out an inefficient programme. Because it is ineffective, or technically inefficient, or not cost-effective, or because its outcomes are not valued enough, we will be devoting too many resources to it — such as doctors — which will be wasted. One of the things about which it is possible to be wasteful is efficiency itself. Because efficiency is costly to identify, monitor and enforce, one has to be efficient at being efficient! Too much efficiency is wasteful!

Fortunately for our purposes, however, we do not yet appear to have anywhere nearly reached the stage when this sobering thought need curb the enthusiasm of those who recognise the important truth that the more efficient we are at meeting needs, the more needs we shall be able to meet.

# 6. Meeting Need Efficiently : Some Case Studies

In this chapter we turn to current planning problems of the NHS with the material of chapter 5 as background. An array of such problems will be presented, some of them large-scale and some of them small-scale. The first set of problems discussed will be concerned with the operating costs of hospitals; second, the cost-effectiveness and cost—benefit comparisons of particular procedures; and third, manpower planning in the NHS.

## I HOSPITAL COSTS

Expenditure on hospitals accounts for about two-thirds of all NHS spending. Not surprisingly it has been a major concern of the DHSS to ensure that they operate in an efficient manner, given whatever needs they may be meeting. Interest at the policy level has been concerned with such questions as the ideal length of stay of in-patient cases, expenditure-minimising size of hospitals (usually defined in terms of beds as a proxy for 'capacity'), the possibility of identifying hospitals that are more or less efficient than others, the effects on cost of differences in the kind of function performed, etc.

There are many problems connected with analysis of these questions. The most general is that hospitals are far from homogeneous: the

61

quality of their treatment varies, their age varies, their location (and hence resource prices) varies, as does the mix of types of case, the degree to which they teach medical students, train nurses, etc. The standard cost unit employed in hospital studies is the case (not, say, cost per patient per week).

The most comprehensive study of NHS hospitals remains that of Feldstein (1967), who proposed methods by which a number of the problems mentioned above could be overcome. One such innovation was to introduce a method of standardising for case mix differences to enable more valid inter-hospital comparisons to be made. In 1960, for example, among large non-teaching acute hospitals, less than 10 per cent of the case load were medical cases in 10 per cent of the hospitals, about 12 per cent of the case load was medical in 18 per cent of the hospitals, while over 30 per cent of the case load was medical in 2 per cent of the hospitals. In surgery and obstetrics the spread was even greater. The essence of Feldstein's procedure for adjusting the crude cost data per case was to compare the crude figure with an estimate of what its costs should be given its case mix. That is, if its costs for each type of case were the same as the national average cost for cases of that type, a predicted cost figure can be derived by applying the actual case proportions of the hospital in question to the nationally average costs per case to derive the *expected* cost per case for that hospital.

An illustration may help to make this clear. Consider three hospitals of the same size but with differing mixes of five alternative case types. The numbers of patients and the average cost per case are given in table 6.1. Thus, hospital A's 100 cases (per year) are distributed among

TABLE 6.1.
*Effects of case mix on cost comparisons*

| Case type | Hospital A cases | Average cost | Hospital B cases | Average cost | Hospital C cases | Average cost | National average cost per case |
|---|---|---|---|---|---|---|---|
| 1 | 10 | 30 | 50 | 60 | 0 | 30 | 30 |
| 2 | 20 | 60 | 10 | 60 | 10 | 60 | 60 |
| 3 | 30 | 90 | 10 | 90 | 10 | 90 | 90 |
| 4 | 20 | 120 | 10 | 120 | 10 | 90 | 120 |
| 5 | 20 | 150 | 10 | 180 | 70 | 120 | 150 |
| Average cost per case | (96) 96 | | (57) 75 | | (132) 108 | | |

the different case types as shown and its own average cost per case type is in the adjacent column. Crude comparisons might indicate that hospital B was the most efficient, hospital A next and hospital C the least efficient, having the highest average cost per case. These comparisons, however, make no allowance for casemix variations. Given its case mix, if hospital B had the same costs per case type as the national average, its average cost per case should have been £57, not £75. This hospital is actually relatively inefficient, taking its case mix into account. Conversely, hospital C would be expected by national norms to have an average cost per case of £132, not £108, indicating that it comes top, not bottom, of the league of three hospitals.

Much refinement has, of course, subsequently gone into the development of empirical measures of case mix, case complexity (see, e.g. Evans and Walker, 1972) etc., and rather sophisticated econometric techniques are commonly used to derive estimates of the effects of the various factors. The results of part of a recent econometric study by the author and some colleagues for hospital data in 1969—70 are presented in table 6.2. By 1972—73, average cost per case had risen to nearly £213 for London teaching hospitals and £125 for all non-teaching hospitals. These results were derived from the following estimated equation:

£ (cost per case) =

$$18.38 + 8.66 \text{ (case complexity)} - 0.378 \text{ (beds)}$$
$$(16.13) \quad (1.89) \quad\quad\quad\quad\quad\quad (0.0144)$$

$$+ 0.000044 \text{ (beds}^2) + 34.50 \text{ (occupancy)} + 4.32 \text{ (length of stay)}$$
$$(0.000017) \quad\quad\quad (18.10) \quad\quad\quad\quad (1.05)$$

$$- 0.404 \text{ (patient throughput)} + 11.98 \text{ (London location)} + 3557 \text{ (students)}$$
$$(0.435) \quad\quad\quad\quad\quad\quad (1.52) \quad\quad\quad\quad\quad\quad (269)$$

Adjusted $R^2 = 0.78$.

TABLE 6.2.
*Predicted and actual average current cost per case in 1969—70 (£)*

|  | Metropolitan regional hospital board hospitals | Provincial regional hospital board hospitals | London teaching hospitals | Provincial teaching hospitals |
|---|---|---|---|---|
| Predicted | 98.75 | 73.15 | 133.55 | 109.51 |
| Actual | 91.08 | 78.96 | 142.88 | 105.96 |

The interpretation of the equation is that the regression coefficients (the numbers preceding the bracketed independent variables) indicate the addition to cost per case attributed to a one unit change in the independent variables (such as case complexity). While the standard errors beneath these coefficients indicate that not all are, from the statistical point of view, significantly different from zero, this particular equation is of interest because it gave the *lowest* estimate of the impact on cost of undergraduate medical students in 1969 out of a whole set of regression results. The student variable indicates that the extra current cost to the NHS (excluding University Grants Committee, or university, costs) was estimated to be at least £3,557 per undergraduate year. Of course, it need not follow that the average student cost is the same as the cost of an *additional* student. Indeed, the equation reveals that there are scale economies in beds, so that larger hospitals will, up to a point, have lower unit costs (see the two terms for beds).

The existence of lower current costs with large size (in terms of beds) has been investigated in several studies of which a sample are indicated in table 6.3.

A recent survey of the hospital cost literature by Berki (1972) concluded sardonically: '. . . depending on the methodologies and definitions used, economics of scale exist, may exist, or do not exist, but in any case, according to theory, they ought to exist'!

Although we cannot survey this literature in any detail, it is valuable to make some general comments about it, some of which refer back to our earlier general discussion. First, the data upon which much

TABLE 6.3.
*Size of hospital for which unit costs are lowest*

| Study | Country | Least cost size (beds) |
|---|---|---|
| Carr and Feldstein (1967) | USA | 190 |
| Feldstein (1967) | UK | 310 or 900* |
| Berry (1967) | USA | no scale economies |
| Cohen (1967a) | USA | 150–350 |
| Cohen (1967b) | USA | 540–700 |
| Ro (1968) | USA | up to 800 |
| Evans and Walker (1972) | Canada | no scale economies |
| Culyer *et al.* | UK | 500 |

*The latter size if the larger hospitals could reduce length of stay to that associated with smaller hospitals.

sophisticated statistical analysis has been done are far from perfect. Second, it is extremely difficult to specify a model correctly; in particular, the definition of output (e.g., quality of care or, ideally, production of increases in health or reductions in the community's need, or the production of knowledge and of teaching) is extremely difficult, as is the accurate specification of inputs. Third, the role of time is rarely made explicit in these studies — are the costs long-term or short-term? When we have discussed cost—benefit analysis later in this chapter, a further question that will arise, but which has rarely been asked, relates to the *present value* of future costs and to the size of hospital that minimises these per case. Fourth, statistical cost studies tend to take efficient technologies for granted. Much of the variability of the results, especially as regards optimal scale, probably reflects the fact that there is very little incentive for hospitals to use the most efficient technique. Rather, their major financial incentive is to spend their budgets — and ask for more! Finally, the cost data used are typically current expenditure data whose relationship to social expenditure, let alone social cost, is rarely explored.

An alternative approach to hospital costs is to use local accounting data supplemented by additional collection of data to analyse the cost of treating specific case types (e.g. Babson, 1973; Mason *et al.*, 1974; Russell, 1974). A characteristic difficulty here is the allocation of joint costs of nursing etc. The simple answer might seem to be to calculate the proportion of nursing time, doctors' time, bed time etc. devoted to, say, the hernia cases. And this is frequently done. Unfortunately, it makes little sense from the point of view of efficiency. It is like asking the question, is the cost of grazing the cost of the mutton or the wool? There is no answer to that. The question to which there is an answer, however, is how much it would cost in extra grazing (and possibly less wool) to produce an extra pound of mutton. But, typically, this type of study does not ask *incremental* questions of this sort.

The general lesson to be learned from all this is, of course, that cost studies should be looked at with one's critical wits about one. An important corollary of this modesty is, however, that one should view with scepticism claims by hospitals that they have increased their 'productivity', that a new project is 'worthwhile', that they are less costly than others, that they need more resources to maintain the 'quality of care' etc. Equally, again, some problems have had an interesting and helpful light shed upon them and the manifest difficulties should not deter the NHS from more intensive research into hospital efficiency.

## II  COST EFFECTIVENESS AND COST−BENEFIT STUDIES

In the cost effectiveness study by Piachaud and Weddell (1972), two alternative procedures for treating varicose veins were examined. Since the medical outcome of each procedure was taken to be the same, the thorny problem of measuring output, to ensure that one really was comparing the relative costs of two technologies for doing the *same* thing was avoided (however, there is some controversy as to whether the outcomes are, in fact, so similar; and, more subtly, the question we turn to in chapter 8, concerning whether the productivity in terms of need reduction might not have been greater with different selections of patients, was not discussed).

Two methods of treating varicose veins are to remove them either by injection-compression sclerotherapy in an out-patient clinic or by surgery as an in-patient. Since injection-compression treatment takes place in special clinics, the costs of an out-patient session were relatively unambiguously identifiable and amounted to £41.50. It was assumed that money outlays measured the relevant dimensions of hospital cost accurately. The average number of patients treated per session was 31 and the average number of attendances per patient was 7.3. The total cost of the procedure per treated patient was thus, on average, £9.77. The estimation of surgical costs was complicated by the substantial amount of resources shared by veins patients with other surgical and medical in-patients (e.g. catering, laundry, administration, nursing). These costs were divided up according to estimates of the relative intensity of their utilisation by veins patients, which, as we have seen, necessarily involves some arbitrariness. The estimated total cost per case was £44.22. The estimated institutional costs of surgery thus substantially exceeded those of injection compression.

Two further dimensions of cost were also considered in this study: time off work and patient time used up in treatment. The average number of days off work owing to treatment and convalescence for surgery was 31.3 days, compared with 6.4 days for injection-compression treatment. As for patient time, allowing for post-operative out-patient attendances and travelling time, surgery cost about 100 hours and injection-compression sclerotherapy about 30 hours. Since these results reinforced the institutional cost results, there was no necessity to express them in monetary units: the cost-effective solution is rather unambiguous. Even with substantial reductions in the in-patient length of stay, surgery appears not to be cost-effective.

Cost differentials of this magnitude occur with surprising frequency among those cost effectiveness studies that have been undertaken in the health service field (see e.g. Klarman *et al.*, 1968) and suggest that, even though some refinements of analysis were not utilised, the results would not be substantially altered: the conceptual difficulties that may intimidate at the *a priori* stage sometimes vanish in the context of practical application of the basic analytical apparatus.

The existence of the submerged 'clinical iceberg', discussed in chapter 3, as well as technological developments and other more general humanistic concerns has led to an increasing demand for mass screening of the relevant populations at risk to identify presymptomatic disease and to cure patients in the early stages. Cervical smear programmes, amniocentesis with abortion for women carrying mongol foetuses and testing for high blood pressure are much talked about screening procedures. But perhaps the best known screening programmed in Britain was the mass miniature radiography (MMR) programme for detection of pulmonary tuberculosis — now, of course, being abandoned on a large scale.

At the end of the 1960s this programme was costing around £1m. per annum — not a large sum by comparison with other expenditure categories, but was it money well spent? The objects of MMR were basically threefold: to identify cases at a stage when they could be 'nipped in the bud'; to tackle part of the submerged clinical iceberg; and to prevent infection of others by those with presymptomatic TB. The cost of finding an active case of pulmonary TB was around £500. The benefits depend upon the probability of secondary infection from primary cases, the time lags involved (time discounting becomes important here), the differential cost of treatment earlier rather than later and the reduction in output resulting from reducing or eliminating disability, prolonged hospitalisation or death.

Today, technological developments in pharmacology imply that drug therapy is almost completely effective, irrespective of the stage of the TB. Disease activity ceases within a few days of the start of treatment. There is little or no cost differential in identifying cases picked up by MMR or symptomatically — and many of those positive cases picked up by MMR would have cured themselves anyway. In recent years there has been an annual rate of decrease in notifications of TB of about 9 per cent per year. The principal potential gain from MMR clearly has to lie in the prevention of secondary cases, if the programme is to be regarded as worthwhile in today's conditions.

Pole (1971), using a 10 per cent discount rate, found the range of potential benefits from finding a case of TB indicated in table 6.4, assuming that MMR works with *maximum* effectiveness by completely eliminating the infectious phase of the disease. On the assumptions that are thus most favourable to MMR, the costs are almost twice the benefits. In a social sense, prevention need not be better than cure, and here is a case in which it appears not to be. The decision to abandon mass screening for pulmonary tuberculosis under the NHS was, it would appear, amply justified.

TABLE 6.4.

*Maximum average present value of finding a TB case by MMR (£)*

|  |  | \multicolumn{3}{c}{Case avoided after:} | | |
|  |  | 10 years | 20 years | 30 years |
| Assumed annual rate | 5% | 285 | 75 | 26 |
| of decline of new |  |  |  |  |
| cases notified | 10% | 181 | 34 | 7 |

*Source:* Pole (1971)

Although the study by Pole uses the word 'benefit', it cannot really be counted a cost–benefit study, for the benefit here is the cost of alternative treatment avoided. Effectively, he was comparing the cost of one procedure (preventive care) with another (remedial care). The benefits, in terms of the social gains from more or less sickness, did not get a look in at all. In fact, the attempts that have been made to value benefits in cost–benefit analyses of health procedures have been extremely crude, not to say vulgar. In the technical economic literature much effort has been expended on identifying the appropriate measure, which is related to the *maximum* amount that persons (including those affected externally by, say, compassion or physically by, say, the risk of infection) would pay to have the specified benefit or, alternatively, the *minimum* that must be paid to forego it supposing it to be on offer 'for free'. The 'benefit' must, of course, relate to a change in a suitably defined health index. Even these apparently clear measures of principle are conceptually far from clear, however (see, e.g. Mishan, 1971), and become doubly difficult when allowance is made for uncertainty and risk. Oddly, the most sophisticated progress in benefit measurement has taken place in the extremely difficult area of the valuation of reductions in the probability of death itself. The most sophisticated of these is Jones-Lee (1976). A less comprehensive measure, but one that attempts accuracy — as far as it goes — is Akehurst and Culyer (1974).

In practice, one sometimes doubts whether some researchers have even heard of the principles of benefit evaluation, quite apart from our obligation to be charitable towards those who have heard of them but, faced with an uncompromising reality, adopt perforce a ruder approximation. One obsession that runs through some studies is to focus on expenditures for benefit evaluation. The case for (or against!) fluoridation of water supplies, for example, is based upon the estimated reduction in the treatment of caries (about 55 per cent reduction in cases), but the costs vary very much according to the size of the population served by a water treatment works; moreover, they do not normally account for the fact that fluoridation tends less to reduce the need for dental services than to change its nature and the time at which the need emerges — with fewer teeth lost or damaged by decay in youth, adults will need more periodontal and maintenance care; and, later on, conservative dentistry is likely to become more necessary as edentulousness is postponed. Setting these complications aside, Davies (1973) valued the reduction in the incidence of caries in terms of the fees for conservative dentistry, extractions etc. charged by US dentists and found a favourable ratio of benefits to costs. Using NHS charges, however, one would tend to conclude that it would be uneconomic to fluoridate some water supplies. Would this be a valid inference?

The answer must be an emphatic 'no'. While fees paid may be a valid measure of part of the actual benefit received by those willing to pay the fees (whether in the UK or the USA), they constitute an underestimate of the total benefit for at least three major reasons. First, what anyone pays for anything is rarely the maximum that could be 'extorted' from him by a monopoly seller (the difference between what he actually pays and the maximum is known as consumer's surplus). Second, many who could benefit may be excluded by having to pay a fee and so, although they *may* value the benefit less than the cost of supplying it to them, (i) we do not know if this is so since fees do not necessarily correspond to the cost of treating an additional patient and (ii) all benefits should be counted anyway. Third, the benefits thus measured exclude the value to individuals of not having extractions, of a life freer of pain by prevention rather than treatment (which may not restore one anyway to one's premorbid state), and also of the general benefits that accrue to members of society who value other people's health for its own sake. At best, therefore, such estimates of benefit are *minimal* estimates which, if they turn out to be less than (social) cost, cannot alone constitute a case against fluoridation (one cannot say it would be 'uneconomic'; one would have to confess that one did not know).

Another obsession on the benefit side — especially in studies of life-saving procedures — is with earnings. One recent study (Buxton and West, 1975) evaluated the benefits in Britain from long-term haemodialysis of people with kidney failure 'in narrow economic terms' by calculating the present value of expected wages of those benefiting from the treatment sufficiently to go to work. More sophisticated studies of benefits (e.g. Weisbrod, 1961) have made adjustments to similar data to allow, e.g., for expected unemployment and future taxation. But in what sense are earnings a benefit from medical care? From the point of view of society other than the patient, he is enabled to engage in productive (we suppose) activity. But for this he is paid and, normally, the wage paid to a marginal worker is approximately the value he adds to production — society thus both receives but also pays and, on the margin, is indifferent. On the worker's side there is indeed some benefit from working (otherwise why work?) and hence some benefit from being enabled to work. However, for most people, a wage is a necessary *compensation for having to work* and only a *part* of his income exceeds this compensation.

These crude attempts to value benefits are thus extremely hazardous, both inasmuch as they may not really be benefits at all and inasmuch as, if they are benefits, how they should be interpreted. In benefit evaluation, as in cost evaluation, great caution and subtlety is required. In an area where even economic sophisticates can, and have been, easily led astray, the hidden mines for the unwary amateur are potentially disastrous. It is worth emphasising too that these indirect ways of benefit measurement are particularly overlaid with hazards. Ultimately there is no avoiding the painstaking path, outlined in chapter 4, of measuring health and changes in health status and then, subsequently, of attaching explicit values and priorities to patients (see chapter 7). This prospect may daunt those in view of the work that remains to be done in this territory, and it may not appeal to those who prefer to have the crucial issues of value in the NHS buried in a fog of obscurantism, but to attach an explicit value to a unit gain in a health index has every prospect of leading to a much more humanitarian and egalitarian NHS. In addition, it has the signal virtue of inviting us to consider, before we ever get down to valuing the outcomes, what precisely these outcomes are.


## III  MANPOWER PLANNING

Is there (was there/will there be) a doctor shortage? It all, of course, depends whom you ask. In the early 1950s the medical profession thought there was not because the middle hospital grades were filling up and the prospects for promotion to consultant grade were, as a matter of arithmetical fact, falling. The GPs too, were worried, because the 'pool' system of payment then used meant that with fewer GPs each would get a larger slice of the pool. In the 1960s, by which time these financial (and career) problems had been in part solved by administration changes, the doctors felt, on the basis of population projections (and other factors) that severe shortages were looming, despite an increase in the number of (hospital) doctors of over 20 per cent from 1955 to 1965 and a stationary GP population. At the time of alleged over-supply, it was also argued of course that remuneration should not be used to regulate the stock.

If you were to ask an egalitarian there would of course invariably be a shortage — for the compelling arithmetic logic that since one cannot easily reduce the number of doctors in areas with a high doctor-to-population ratio, one must increase the number of doctors in those areas below the average.

The answer to the question thus does depend upon whom you ask — and when you ask him. If you ask an economist, however, he will again say that it all depends: in particular, it depends upon what you are aiming to do and how many doctors you have to do it. Some economists would argue that you cannot define a shortage without reference to market prices. That is, at best, a half-truth. It is true that at certain prices individuals may demand more than suppliers are prepared to supply, so that queues develop and rationing devices supplementing price have to be employed. This is a useful *behavioural* notion of shortage. For evaluative purposes, however, we need a definition that transcends the particular institutions a society may use to allocate its resources, for it may be that we shall wish to identify shortages in a *normative* sense where there are none in the behavioural sense in the market, or to assert that there is no shortage when, in the non-market sector, we observe queues. While shortages in the normative sense cannot be identified without assigning values to resources and expected outcomes, they can most certainly be identified without using market prices; for these can, as we have seen, give misleading information about the true social costs and benefits. Thus, a shortage exists, as we have defined it above, when a programme that is *worth* doing cannot be done as planned because of insufficient resources. The same definition applies in the present and in the future – but in the future, of course, the many problems deriving from uncertainty are much multiplied. The thing that is worth doing must, of course, be defined independently of the number of doctors: the NHS does not exist, according to this book, to give employment to doctors, but to give effective care to patients. Since doctors are sometimes (but not invariably) a necessary input to this end, any statement about shortage, whether current or anticipated, must derive from their role as a means of achieving this end.

So much may seem platitudinous, yet, while we can all readily acknowledge the great difficulties in measuring such a notion of shortage, much of NHS manpower planning appears not to acknowledge that such a definition can be the only relevant touchstone for devising manpower policies.

Manpower planning is less an on-going process in the UK than the subject of *ad hoc* reviews from time to time, usually in response to a crisis, either real or imagined. The first such review was Willink (1957), a committee established in 1955 to predict future doctor requirements and the appropriate, earlier, throughput of medical students.

The Willink report has been widely cited as a classic of bad manpower forecasting. Their procedure was to determine the existing number of doctors in practice and to estimate the replacements required through to 1971 owing to death and retirement. Adjustment was then made for population increase (to maintain present ratios), for net migration of doctors, and for the demand for doctors in the armed forces, universities, etc. Some consideration was also given to technology change and current 'deficiencies'. On grounds of the unpredictability of the former no adjustment was made, but target levels of GPs were set with respect to the latter of 2,500 patients per principal GP in urban and 2,000 in rural areas. Hospital specialist demand estimates were clouded in mystery, though ratios of junior and senior staff were to be maintained.

The upshot of all these considerations was a recommendation to reduce medical school intake by 10 per cent. By October 1957 medical school intake was down by 10 per cent. It soon became clear that the Willink conclusions were highly sensitive to changes in the assumptions. Lafitte and Squire (1960), by using the revised official population forecast of 8 per cent growth (instead of the 4 per cent given to Willink) and a revision of retirement estimates, estimated that 1971 requirements had been understated by about 17 per cent. They also queried the assumption that standards of care should not increase along with real incomes and the conservative assumptions about emigration of doctors, even though the Pilkinton Report on doctors' and dentists' remuneration in 1960 was still confident that doctor emigration was only 'average'. Later studies (e.g. Abel-Smith and Gales, 1964; Gish, 1971; Kilgour, 1971) confirmed that emigration was running higher than average — though by not as much as some had reported.

Paige and Jones's (1965, 1966) unofficial forecasts of shortage in 1985 were based on types of calculation similar to those of Willink, allowing notably for changes in the balance of community and institutional care (especially for the mentally ill). The Todd Report (1968) was the next official foray into medical futurology. Basically the same method was used as by Willink, though with reliance placed upon the new regional hospital board reviews instituted since the Platt Report on hospital career structures (Platt, 1961). This methodology consists essentially of selecting one single 'best' estimate and (in Todd) reached a new high tide of absurdity. Although their long-term estimates for 1995 were put forward with suitable modesty, they were much taken by the fact that a line with an exponential growth rate of 1.25 per cent, relating the doctor—population ratio to time, passed close to the actual values of 1911 and 1961 as well as through their estimate for 1975. Since the 1965 ratio, however, lay below the line, 1965 was identified as a year of shortage.

It is, of course, churlish to criticise the manpower planners for having taken as data the wrong estimates supplied to them by the Registrar General. Likewise, it is churlish to criticise them for being wrong about facts where no data existed (for example, the actual number of hospital doctors has at all times been higher than predicted requirements because immigration of doctors has been running at an unpredicted 3,000 per year compared with emigration of about 300).

There are, however, more substantial criticisms. The first is that manpower planning is not, and never has been, integrated properly into the planning of the NHS. Unless and until a more sensitive and systematic inquiry is regularly made into the future needs that are planned to be met by the NHS, then the manpower planners can do little more than rely on forecasts of population and its composition by age and sex and assume (explicitly or implicitly) that the needs met now will continue to be met in the future and in basically the same way.

The evidence, though it is of a preliminary sort (Lavers and Whynes, 1975), suggests that manpower productivity growth has been extremely small, or negative, at least from 1960 to 1970, as table 6.5 reveals. Unfortunately, results on labour productivity as compared with the average of all factors in the hospital service are not yet available, nor have similar calculations been done for other parts of the health service. What is clear, however, is that the prices of various components in the total varied greatly over the decade. By fiscal 1970—71 doctors' salaries, for example, had more than doubled, while drugs and dressings had actually fallen. Thus, while the aggregate picture given in table 6.5 tends to support the working assumption in forecasting exercises that productivity, in so far as it can be measured at all, does not increase in the hospital sector, it is a rather depressing assumption to have to make. A better assumption, however, will have to await the results of further examination of individual factor productivity, of past trends in factor substitution of various kinds and of planned substitution over the planning period.

Of course, manpower planning need not take always the very long view when the uncertainties are at their largest, even in the case of doctors who take six years in the training. Though medical school planning may require longish periods, the supply of doctors and nurses is also very much determined by migration to and from Britain and, in the shorter term, there is no reason to suppose that manipulation of pay scales would not have an important role to play. Unfortunately there is no study of the medium-term supply elasticity of medical manpower, i.e. estimation of the ratio of the percentage net change in manpower to the percentage change in (real or current) income.

Although the method of remuneration of doctors is complex, it is perfectly amenable to appropriate manipulations of this sort. In the GP primary care sector one would hazard the guess that the medium-term elasticity is very low (most doctors who emigrate, for example, seem to be frustrated junior hospital doctors) but we have little information on the degree to which students in training change their plans regarding

## TABLE 6.5.
### Indices of hospital average productivity, 1960 = 100

| | 1961 | 1962 | 1963 | 1964 | 1965 | 1966 | 1967 | 1968 | 1969 | 1970 |
|---|---|---|---|---|---|---|---|---|---|---|
| Crude productivity Index (1) (deaths and discharges) | 100.5 | 101.4 | 103.9 | 104.6 | 102.9 | 101.2 | 100.1 | 99.7 | 98.8 | 96.4 |
| crude productivity Index (2) (with out-patient attendances) | 101.1 | 99.7 | 102.3 | 103.6 | 101.0 | 99.7 | 98.9 | 97.8 | 97.5 | 95.7 |
| social productivity | 101.6 | 102.7 | 105.7 | 107.1 | 105.5 | 104.7 | 103.6 | 103.0 | 103.2 | 101.5 |
| Economic output index (i) at 5% discount rate | | | | 100 | 97.3 | 92.3 | 92.9 | 91.3 | 93.0 | 87.9 |
| (ii) at 10% discount rate | | | | 100 | 97.3 | 92.3 | 92.8 | 91.3 | 92.7 | 87.6 |
| (iii) at 15% discount rate | | | | 100 | 97.2 | 92.2 | 92.8 | 91.3 | 92.6 | 87.5 |

Source: calculated from table 4 in Lavers and Whynes (1975).

primary or hospital practice. GPs' pay is made up principally of capitation fees for patients on their lists who are under sixty-five, over sixty-five and in excess of 1,000. There are then supplementary payments for, e.g., a basic practice allowance, out-of-hours duties, night visits, vaccinations, whether or not the practice is located in a 'designated' (i.e. 'under-doctored') area or where lists per doctor exceed 3,000. Plainly, the capitation fees are the element most suited to variation, and allowance would have to be made for the fact that changing the number of doctors changes list sizes and hence earnings from the capitation system.

In the hospital sector, where most in and out migration occurs, the elasticity is likely to be substantially higher (we must not take too seriously the polite professional view expressed by most emigrants from the hospital service that work conditions were the principal determining factor in their decision). The hospital doctor moves from house officer to senior house officer, registrar and senior registrar to the position of consultant, whose salaries are on a nine-point scale. Many are part-time, spending (officially) not more than nine-elevenths of their working sessions in the NHS, with the rest of their time free for private practice. In addition there are Distinction Awards carrying substantial (and permanent) financial rewards of which about 30 per cent of hospital doctors are in receipt.

To the extent, however, that we accept the requirements estimated by the manpower planners in the past, it is ironic to note that, while the Willink hospital doctor requirements estimated for 1965 and 1970 were — as is, of course, to be expected — well exceeded in actuality, the Paige and Jones requirements for 1980 were passed already in 1973 and even the Todd requirements for 1975 were equalled in 1973.

The story so far is essentially one pointing to the need for much greater research into planning co-ordination, needs assessment, productivity and substitution measurement and the measurement (not merely the description) of behavioural response by doctors to various parameters of (individual) behaviour — especially, of course, rates of pay. In an area fraught with uncertainty, there is also an overwhelming case for the use of alternative assumptions to test the sensitivity of the forecasts.

More radically, we may consider on grounds of equity the whole question of the financing of medical education. Currently, the state finances a large part of the cost of educating and training doctors via local authority grants for living, by grants to the universities and (see the suggestive results on costs earlier in this chapter) via additional (hidden) costs imposed on the NHS. The major cost for the student is his foregone earnings. These represent very substantial subsidies to people who some day are going to be substantially better off than most members of society, and an investment whose return is lost if the individual, having received his training, decides to use it overseas by emigrating. In fact, the investment is a very profitable one for the individual even if he does not emigrate, the most recent estimate yielding a rate of return of about 20 per cent *after* tax (Walker, 1974).

It is increasingly becoming recognised that the finance of higher education in general may be better done on the basis of some version of a repayable loan to students or a 'graduate tax' (see, e.g., Prest, 1966; Peacock and Wiseman, 1964, 1966). The loan idea, coupled with more realistic fee-setting in higher education, would have the great advantage of shifting some of the risks of investment in medical manpower to the relatively highly paid people who are currently shielded from them by society in general. The risks, of course, of lower than expected earnings or non-available posts of the sort desired would be not much more under the alternative arrangement than they are now but, in the event that a doctor decided that opportunities in Britain were too poor for him relative to those abroad, at least the State's investment in him would no longer be lost.

## BIBLIOGRAPHY

Abel-Smith, B. and Gales, K. (1964) *British Doctors at Home and Abroad* London, Bell

Adler, M. W. *et al.* (1974) 'A Randomised Control Trial of Early Discharge for Inguinal Hernia and Varicose Veins — some problems of methodology', *Medical Care*, vol. 12

Akehurst, R. L. and Culyer, A. J. (1974) 'On the Economic Surplus and the Value of Life' *Bulletin of Economic Research*, vol. 26

Ashely, J. S. A., Howlett, A. and Morris, J. N. (1971) 'Case Fatality of Hyperplasia of the Prostrate in two Teaching and three Regional Board Hospitals' *Lancet* (ii)

Babson, J. (1973) *Disease Costing* Manchester, University Press

Beckerman, W. (1965) *The British Economy in 1975* Cambridge, University Press.

Berki, S. E. (1972) *Hospital Economics* Lexington, D.C. Heath

Berry, R. E. (1967) 'Returns to Scale in the Production of Hospital Services' *Health Services Research*, Summer

Boulding, K. E. (1954) 'An Economist's View of the Manpower Concept' in National Manpower Council, *Proceedings of a Conference on the Utilization of Scientific and Professional Manpower* New York, Columbia University Press

Buxton, M. J. and West, R. R. (1975) 'Cost–benefit Analysis of Long-term Haemodialysis for Chronic Renal Failure' *British Medical Journal*, 17 May

Carr, W. J. and Feldstein, P. (1967) 'The Relationship of Cost to Hospital Size' *Inquiry*, June

Cochrane, A. L. (1972) *Effectiveness and Efficiency: random reflections on health services* London, Nuffield Provincial Hospitals Trust

Cohen, H. A. (1967a) 'Variations in Cost Among Hospitals of Different Sizes' *Southern Economic Journal*, January

Cohen, H. A. (1967b) 'Costs and Efficiency: a study of short-term general hospitals, PhD dissertation (unpublished), Cornell University

Cooper, M. H. (1975) *Rationing Health Care* London, Croom Helm

Cooper, M. H. and Culyer, A. J. (eds) (1973) *Health Economics* London, Penguin

Culyer, A. J. and Maynard, A. K. (1970) 'The Costs of Dangerous Drugs Legislation in England and Wales' *Medical Care*, vol. 8

Davies, G. N. (1973) 'Fluoride in the prevention of dental caries: a tentative cost–benefit analysis' *British Dental Journal*, 21 August

de Dombal, F. T. *et al.* (1972) 'Computer-aided Diagnosis of Acute Abdominal Pain' *British Medical Journal*, Vol. 2, 1 April

Elwood, P. C. and Pitman, R. G. (1966) 'Observer Error in the Radiological Diagnosis of Paterson-Kelly Webs' *British Journal of Radiology*, vol. 39

Evans, R. G. and Walker, H. (1972) 'Information Theory and the Analysis of Hospital Cost Structure' *Canadian Journal of Economics*, vol. 5

Feldstein, M. S. (1967) *Economic Analysis for Health Service Efficiency* Amsterdam, North Holland

Gish, O. (1971) *Doctor Migration and World Health* London, Bell

Jacobs, P. (1974) 'A Survey of Economic Models of Hospitals' *Inquiry*, vol. 9

Jones-Lee, M. (1976) *The Value of Life: An economic analysis* London, Martin Robertson.

Kilgour, J. (1971) 'Migration of Doctors and Medical Manpower Planning' *Health Trends*, vol. 3

Klarman, H. E. (1965) 'Syphilis Control Programs' in R. Dorfman (ed) *Measuring Benefits of Government Investments* Washington D.C., Brookings Institution

Klarman, H. E. *et al.* (1968) 'Cost Effectiveness Applied to the Treatment of Chronic Renal Disease' *Medical Care*, vol. 6 (reprinted in Cooper and Culyer, 1973)

Klarman, H. E. (1969) 'Economic Aspects of Projecting Requirements for Health Manpower' *Journal of Human Resources*, vol. 4

Klarman, H. E. (ed.) (1970) *Empirical Studies in Health Economics* Baltimore and London, Johns Hopkins Press

Klarman, H. E. (1974) 'Application of Cost–Benefit Analysis to the Health Services and the Special Case of Technological Innovation' *International Journal of Health Services*, vol. 4

Lafitte, F. and Squire, J. R. (1960) 'Second thoughts on the Willink Report' *Lancet*, 3 September

Lavers, R. J. and Whynes, D. (1975) 'Hospital Productivity Trends in the

Swinging Sixties', paper given at the Health Economists' Study Group Meeting in July 1975

Lee, J. A. H. *et al.* (1963) 'Case-fatality in Teaching and Non-teaching Hospitals 1956—59' *Medical Care*, vol. 1

Mason, A. M. S. *et al.* (1974) 'Disease Costing in Hospitals', introductory paper for a one-day symposium held at Northwick Park Hospital, unpublished

Maynard, A. K. and Walker, A. (1975) 'Medical Manpower Planning in the UK: a critical appraisal', unpublished.

McKeown, T. (1971) 'A Historical Appraisal of the Medical Task' in T. McKeown *et al.*, *Medical History and Medical Care* London, Oxford University Press for the Nuffield Provincial Hospitals Trust

McKeown, T. and Record, R. G. (1962) 'Reasons for the Decline of Mortality in England and Wales during the Nineteenth Century' *Population Studies*, vol. 16

McKeown, T., Brown, R. G. and Record, R. G. (1972) 'An Interpretation of the Modern Rise of Population in Europe' *Population Studies*, vol. 26.

Mishan, E. J. (1971) *Cost—Benefit Analysis* London, Allen and Unwin

Office of Health Economics (1964) *New Frontiers in Health* London, OHE

Office of Health Economics (1971) *Prospects in Health* London, OHE

Office of Health Economics (1971) *Hypertension: a suitable case for treatment* London, OHE

Office of Health Economics (1972) *Medicine and Society* London, OHE

Paige, D. C. and Jones, K. (1965) 'Health and Welfare' in Beckerman (1965).

Paige, D. C. and Jones, K. (1966) *Health and Welfare Services in Britain in 1975* Cambridge, University Press

Peacock, A. T. and Robertson, D. J. (1963) *Public Expenditure: Appraisal and Control* London, Oliver and Boyd

Peacock, A. T. and Shannon, J. R. (1968) 'The New Doctors' Dilemma' *Lloyds Bank Review*, January

Peacock, A. T. and Wiseman, J. (1964) *Education for Democrats* London, Institute of Economic Affairs

Peacock, A. T. and Wiseman, J. (1966) 'Economic Growth and the principles of educational finance in developed countries' in *Financing of Education for Economic Growth* Paris, OECD

Piachaud, D. and Weddell, J. M. (1972) 'The Economics of Treating Varicose Veins' *International Journal of Epidemiology*, vol. 3

Pilkington Report (1960) *Royal Commission on Doctors' and Dentists' Remuneration: Report* London, HMSO

Platt Report (1961) *Report of the Joint Working Party on the Medical Staffing Structure of the Hospital Service* London, HMSO

Pole, D. (1971) 'Mass Radiography: A Cost-Benefit Approach' in G. McLachlan (ed.) *Problems and Progress in Medical Care 5* Oxford, University Press

Pole, D. (1972) 'The Economics of Mass Radiography' in M. M. Hauser (ed.) *The Economics of Medical Care* London, Allen and Unwin

Prest, A. R. (1966) *Financing University Education* London, Institute of Economic Affairs

Razzell, P. E. (1965) 'Population Change in Eighteenth Century England: a reinterpretation' *Economic History Review*, vol. 18

Razzell, P. E. (1974) 'An Interpretation of the Modern Rise of Population in Europe — A Critique' *Population Studies*, vol. 28

Ro, K. (1968) 'Determinants of Hospital Costs', *Yale Economic Essays*

Rosser, R. and Watts, V. (1975) 'Disability. A clinical classification' *New Law Journal*, 3 April

Russell, E. M. (1974) *Patient Costing Studies* Scottish Health Services Studies No. 31, Scottish Home and Health Department

Sainsbury Report (1967), *Report of the Committee of Enquiry into the Relationship of the Pharmaceutical Industry with the NHS, 1965—67* London, HMSO

Todd Report (1968) *Report of the Royal Commission on Medical Education 1965—68*, Cmd. 3569, London, HMSO

Wadsworth, M. E. J., Butterfield, W. J. H. and Blaney, R. (1971) *Health and Sickness: the choice of treatment* London, Tavistock Institute

Wager, R. (1972) *Care of the Elderly* London, Institute of Treasurers and Municipal Accountants

Walker, A. (1974) 'Manpower in the National Health Service (doctors)', paper given at the Health Economists' Study Group at the University of Kent at Canterbury, 1974

Weisbrod, B. A. (1961) *The Economics of Public Health* Philadelphia, University of Pennsylvania Press

Williams, A. (1974) 'The Cost—Benefit Approach' *British Medical Bulletin*, vol. 3

Williams, A. and Anderson, R. (1975) *Efficiency in the Social Services* London, Basil Blackwell and Martin Robertson

Willink Report (1957) *Report of the Committee to Consider the Future Numbers of Medical Practitioners and the Appropriate Intake of Medical Students* London, HMSO

Wiseman, J. (1963) 'Cost—benefit analysis and health service policy' in Peacock and Robertson (1963)

# 7. Need and the Market Debate

Academic as well as political and professional discussions of the rival merits of price in the market place or queues in the no-price state system as ways of discriminating among rival claimants on the nation's health care resources are notable for the production of much heat and disappointingly little light. Indeed, as will be argued later in this chapter, most of these arguments have entirely missed the boat by virtue of their having failed satisfactorily to face up to the meaning of need and the objectives of the health care system. Before turning to these arguments let us review briefly two major approaches to issues of fairness and equity that have been used by social scientists.

The utilitarian approach is most characteristic of the way in which issues of redistribution and fairness are handled. The objective in utilitarian ethics is to maximise the sum total of the satisfaction experienced by the individuals who collectively form the society in question. In distributive justice, this has implied weighting the satisfaction expressed by (or attributed to) individuals in their acquisition or ownership of a range of goods (including 'good health', privileges, etc., as well as the more everyday economic goods), by the 'marginal utility' of their incomes. Since it is also assumed that the marginal utility of a rich man's income is lower than that of a poor man, the argument both accords its blessing to giving the pound votes of the poor a higher weight than those of the rich and justifies direct money transfers from rich to poor (in principle, until marginal utilities of income are equalised). The quintessential non-observability of marginal utilities of income has led, however, to the invention of a mythical omniscient observer who, somehow, makes the necessary interpersonal comparisons.

Subsequent attempts have been made to overcome the weakness of this fictional character (e.g. by Lerner, 1944), but the fundamental weakness of the utilitarian approach — that its egalitarianism requires a particular pattern of marginal utilities to exist — has never been overcome. If these marginal utilities were actually observable, and if they were *higher* for the rich man than for the poor, then utilitarianism leads us in a direction precisely away from equality or for compensating weights on the comsumption of all goods consumed by the poor. Since equality is such a basic component in most acceptable notions of justice (equality before the law; equality in access to life-saving health care, etc.) this is a most unsatisfactory feature of utilitarianism.

An alternative view which is currently receiving much attention is that associated with the Harvard moral philosopher John Rawls (Rawls, 1972). Rawls argues that conceptions of justice are much conditioned by the positions in society occupied by the individuals holding those conceptions. He postulates a version of social contract theory that requires individuals to ask themselves about the characteristics of a fair society when they are themselves behind a 'veil of ignorance'; i.e., they are to imagine themselves not knowing what social positions they will occupy in society. He argues that individuals will, in these circumstances (viz. behind the veil of ignorance) be absolutely risk-averse and will seek to maximise the wellbeing of the least advantaged member of society. In particular, the two ethical principles of interest here that he derives are: (i) that each person is to have an equal right to the most extensive total system of equal basic liberties comparable with a similar system of liberty for all, and (ii) that social and economic inequalities are to be arranged so that they are to the greatest benefit of the least advantaged.

Now, setting aside some of the difficulties inherent in Rawls's argument (one of which is the implausibility of assuming absolute risk aversion behind the veil of ignorance when individuals are plainly not absolutely risk-averse in normal life), we have here some implications that accord much more with the general feelings that people seem to share about issues involving 'fairness'. This approach also has the virtue of treating fairness as an explicit end itself, rather than — as in utilitarianism — a means to the maximisation of 'satisfaction'. Since the opportunity to plan and live one's life in the way one prefers is a rather basic, and equal, right of all, it follows that access to effective health care procedures that further this end (and, clearly, poor health can destroy one's ability to live, to plan to live and to plan to live satisfactorily) should also be equal. Any deviation, in the Rawlsian scheme, can be regarded as just only if the privileges granted to some have the effect of improving the lot of the more disadvantaged sections of the community. It is hard to think of many persuasive examples of such justifiable privilege in access to effective health care.

Where we might depart from Rawls, however, is in his strict 'lexicographic' ordering of matters of justice over matters of efficiency, such that the former are always prior. It seems to be possible to make a plausible case for modification of the strict egalitarianism of the Rawlsian result on grounds of efficiency. Thus, one could have a kind of utilitarian trade-off between fairness and efficiency. For example, while it would certainly be unfair to put a poor sick man at a disadvantage compared with a rich sick man, we could imagine circumstances in which the rich sick man who had high social productivity should receive more favourable treatment in access to hospital treatment than the poor man without such productivity, for incomes are but a crude indicator (to the extent that they are any kind of indicator) of the value of a person's services to the economy, let alone to, say, their family or to the community in general. This is merely to assert, of course, that neither justice nor efficiency is an absolute value dominating any other, whereas Rawls would say that justice dominates all. One cannot, however, assert what the relative weights should be: this is a matter for public policy. In general, it seems safe to infer that the ethic of the NHS implies a rather high weight on fairness and equality in allocating care among individuals. Unlike Rawls, however, we do not take the view in this book that issues of pure justice must invariably dominate other issues such as those involved in seeking greater efficiency. Indeed there are some forms of 'social productivity', such as 'earning a living for one's dependants', that could readily be incorporated in a just principle for distribution on the grounds that to do so would protect the interests of those dependants.

With this as background let us quickly review the *general* arguments for using waiting time as a means of discriminating between those who express a demand for health care resources. (It is not, of course, the only one. In some instances — emergency cases, for example — it is fortunately very rarely used, with medical judgement being the main factor.) We shall then turn to the arguments against the use of pricing. Finally, having expressed disagreement with almost everyone else who has thought about these problems, we shall present what seems to be the most tenable position.

Time *is* widely used in the NHS to deter users. One waits to see a GP in his surgery (often even if he has an appointment system, and even if you don't wait long you pay another way by getting to see him for the shorter period he can spare you — in a recent survey only 11 per cent of GPs devoted more than six minutes to each patient during consulting hours, and six minutes is not long to make a careful diagnosis, prognosis, to prescribe, to comfort and reassure); one waits for an out-patient appointment to see a hospital doctor; one waits in the out-patient department itself; and one waits, often, for admission to hospital as an in-patient.

A standard utilitarian-type argument for the use of time as a discriminator is that, since time is differently distributed from money income or wealth, it provides a more equitable basis for discrimination between patients than money prices (Nichols, Smolensky and Tideman, 1971; Smolensky, Tideman and Nichols, 1972). The argument runs thus: waiting is most costly for those whose time is the most valuable and these persons are those with high earned incomes. Those with low earning power face lower 'real' prices for access to medical care. Therefore, allocation by waiting discriminates more in favour of the poorer sections of the community.

Several points may be made against this argument for the equity of 'time prices' relative to money prices. First, the discrimination, if it exists, is only against high *earners*; low earners with large 'unearned' income or inherited wealth may be more favourably selected in such a system than low earners who have no other source of income or wealth. Second, the deterrent effect depends not only upon the implicit *money* cost imposed upon waiting patients, but also upon the value, *as they perceive it*, of the money supposedly foregone by waiting. It is possible, though we have no scientific way of knowing it to be so, that the utility of a pound of income foregone by a poor man may, to him, be greater than the utility of fifty pounds of income foregone by a rich man is to him. If so (and this kind of argument is often adduced as an argument for income redistribution from the rich to the poor), then queues will still discriminate against the poor (though less so, of course, than if each had to pay a money price of, say, £50).

More important, however, is the consideration that, though one should not go so far as to assert that the income and wealth characteristics of patients are unimportant in allocating in-patient health care resources, their relevance should, contrary to the utilitarians, be mainly indirect. Justice would seem really to require that the receipt of medical care in the NHS should be wholly independent of income (not systematically related to either low or high incomes) but should be determined by a combination of characteristics, only some of which may be related to income or wealth. The first of these should be whether or not an effective and accepted régime of care exists. Second, the clinical urgency of the case should be a factor. Third, the consequences of delaying access to care should be assessed in terms of the *total* characteristics of the patient in question. These characteristics should include, among other things, the suffering and inconvenience likely to be borne by the patient while waiting; the inconvenience resulting to him or to dependants and relations and the suitability of the home in caring for a sick person, and well as the likely interruption of work, school and the enjoyment of leisure time. If this more comprehensive view of the elements that should be included in a *fair* policy of allocating medical care resources is accepted, then the general inadequacy of the ethical basis of the earned-income method of discrimination is apparent.

This is a specific instance of the general inadequacy of economists' (and others') treatments of issues of equity. By focusing excessively upon income distributions, which are, of course, of great importance in matters concerning the exercise of political, economic and other more subtle sorts of influence and power, the impression is often given that if only the 'problem' of income distribution could be solved, all else is merely a matter for efficiency analysis. As we shall see, this general view seems to have been accepted by rival factions in the 'market versus the state' debate. But it should be clear that a full consideration of the duality of man as both a resource *and* the end-object of social organisation requires us to go far beyond that. Indeed, in the health care sector it almost seems more reasonable to ignore income distributional effects *altogether* and to focus exclusively upon the need for health services. As we have seen in chapter 3, however, income deficiencies are but one of a set of factors appearing to cause poor health (a low demand for health). It is altogether more satisfactory to approach the problem of need directly rather than indirectly through but one of its hypothesised causes. Failure to do so made much of the 'market versus the state' debate somewhat sterile, just as failure to do so has left the NHS in a situation in which efficiency and fairness in reducing need are largely inoperational objectives given the current state of the art.

It is worth noting also that, in principle, the framework of the NHS is ideally suited to the operation of a truly comprehensive attitude to fairness in the allocation of medical care, even though we had some rather critical comments to make in chapter 5 about the 'managerial' discretion enjoyed by the medical profession whose responsibility it is, of course, to make the day-to-day decisions about who shall wait and for how long.

Whether or not this wider conception of the components of a fair allocation between patients existed in the minds of the founding fathers of the NHS is a moot point. Fortunately, for our purposes we need not explore that possibility. It is however a remarkable fact that the ideological debates about the NHS have scarcely discussed a relevant conception of fairness at all. Instead, they have tended to discuss a curious mixture of equity and efficiency arguments, with liberal injections of more or less arbitrary and personal value judgements. Only recently has an interesting way of treating both equity and efficiency at the same time been developed. It still remains to make operational, for the sake of a better NHS, some of these newer ideas — we shall be exploring some of the possibilities in later chapters.

In Britain the long process of banishing a rather smug and complacent attitude to the NHS, at least from academic circles, was begun in 1960 by Dennis Lees in the *Lloyds Bank Review* (Lees, 1960). Lees argued forcibly that medical care appeared to have no uniquely special features that warranted the special kind of arrangements adopted in the UK in the NHS. Chief among these arrangements were the absence of money prices and government ownership of the hospitals.

The reasons often given for the desirability of removing prices to consumers in the health services can be summarised thus: that many individuals, though sick, do not seek treatment because they are deterred by the price (which could, in the case of some kinds of hospital care, be very costly indeed); that uncertainty, fear and ignorance pervade the consumer's attitude to health care consumption anyway and that rational responses to price changes are not to be expected; that there are important side effects of health care consumption, chief of which is the danger of untreated communicable disease which exists because an individual, in reckoning his own advantage from being (say) immunised, will fail to reckon the advantage *to others* of his being immunised and hence will fail to take sufficient precautions.

As regards state ownership, the prevailing attitude that Lees attacked held that profit-seeking by private enterprise hospitals was sordid and debasing, while private charitable foundations were arbitrarily located, lacked the rationality that central planning could bring both as regards situation and the balance of care provided, and were anyway dolers out of charity in a society where it might reasonably be thought that good health should be equally available, as of right, to all individuals, rather than available at the discretion of private charitable institutions.

The attack was a veritable broadside on the sloppiness of thinking that, in truth, usually did accompany these views. Thus, Lees argued that the fact that many sick individuals were deterred by price was only a part of the story, for they were deterred by many other things too, such as fear and ignorance. In any case, granted that some potential clients were deterred by a price, the sensible procedure would be to ensure that satisfactory insurance arrangements were available for everyone so that the system would be more or less self-sustaining on the financial side. Selective subsidies could be made available for those to whom the insurance premiums might prove a heavy burden, but the present system by which the healthy poor subsidised the rich sick was needlessly inefficient as well as unfair. Moreover, the present system, in which an almost unlimited potential demand at zero price could not be met out of very limited tax and publicly borrowed finance, implied that not all demands would or could be met anyway. The insurance system would enable the patient a choice of the kind of care he wanted, the choice of doctor he wanted and the choice of hotel facilities in hospital that he wanted (and not only the very rich have a preference for privacy etc. when sick, for which they would be prepared to pay); whereas in the present system, if you were middle class, articulate and/or happened to live next door to a doctor, you could gain substantial advantages from the system, otherwise everyone could either take or leave whatever the system chose to offer them.

Uncertainty was not unique to health matters and it was a general characteristic of most uncertain events that they were insurable. More important, perhaps, were chronically ill patients, whose future demands were highly certain and hence uninsurable: only for this more limited set of persons, and for immunisation, could there be any case for direct subsidy. It will be apparent by now that the NHS critics' attack on conventional thinking was cast very much in the utilitarian mould which we have briefly described above. In their approach to the ownership question the liberal tradition in utilitarianism came to the fore.

State ownership came under fierce attack. Instead of subsidising *consumers*, who would then be free to select the kind and quality (as they perceived it) of care they wished, having taken whatever technical advice they chose to take, the present system subsidised the *institutions*. GPs were paid roughly according to the number of patients registered with them rather than to the quality of care they gave, so they had little incentive to act in the most effective way for their patients. Moreover, on the one hand, patients, though legally having the right to choose their doctor, frequently had difficulty finding a new doctor in a given locality, especially if they had acquired the reputation in the medical fraternity of being 'difficult'; on the other, the supply of doctors was constrained by the number of places made available in the (state-owned) medical schools and by the remuneration terms agreed between the profession and the State. Thus, there was a double assault on the possibility of supply responding to patient demand. The quality and kind of care to be provided were decisions monopolised in this system by the medical profession, not by the patient who was thus left at the mercy of the professional ethics of the medical men — and everyone knows how difficult it is to demonstrate gross incompetence by having one expert doctor testify against another, let alone to demonstrate minor discourtesy, carelessness or inefficiency.

As may be expected from such strong stuff, the controversy waxed strong and often degenerated into *ad hominem* arguments and irrelevancies (such as whether the US system was 'better' or 'worse' than the British). Since the dust of the battleground has now mostly settled (for those interested in reliving events, the bibliography at the end of this chapter provides a conspectus), we are in the fortunate position today of being able to see what remains of the two extreme positions that is still valid.

One advantage that we have with hindsight derives from the naivety of the arguments concerning the spill-over effects of health care. It is, of course, true that some means of encouraging individuals to prevent their being carriers of a communicable disease is normally necessary if the population is to receive the ideal degree of protection from this source, where the ideal is determined by a balancing of the additional costs of extra protection against the anticipated gains. This had always been recognised by all parties to the debate. On the other hand, the overwhelming part of the NHS's services do not fall into the category of prevention of communicable disease and so this argument plainly will not do as a general argument for the NHS kind of structure of health service delivery.

A much more important kind of effect, which, remarkably enough, went completely unnoticed by both sides, is that the emphasis placed by NHS defenders on the burden of costs on the poor was really another kind of spill-over, which their emphasis on the distribution of income in general blurred. After all, as the critics argued, if one is concerned with the poor, then the poor have major problems in all respects (housing, schooling, clothing, feeding) and not merely in health: the proper answer must be to redistribute incomes to lift the poor out of poverty. Indeed, it was argued, to make free health care available because some families are poor tends to encourage the delusion that poverty will, in some sense, matter less, and hence defer the day when a proper income distribution can be attained. In short, if the poor have too little money, give them the cash.

While this seems a more acceptable — and more radical — approach than that of the NHS defenders, it fails, however, to identify a more crucial thread in the problem — a thread that was never disentangled by the NHS defenders and hence was never subject to the same blast of rational scepticism by the critics. This crucial thread is the spill-over to which reference was made above. The spill-over consists in this: one individual is not affected merely by the possibility of another passing some disease on to him (the traditional spill-over effect) but also, and much more importantly, by the state of health of the other in itself. Individuals are affected by others' health status for the simple reason that *most of them care.* At the most obvious level, most people profoundly object to the thought that *other people's* children may suffer and possibly die because of those others' failure to give them adequate care. Similarly, they object to the plight that elderly sick people may find themselves in. Indeed, more generally, the state of health of others is itself an object of interest to all.

There is of course a distributional issue here, but it is not particularly concerned with income but with health: one feels concerned for the rich sick person because he is sick; one feels concerned for the poor sick person because he is sick and because he is poor. To associate compassion and concern only with the poorer sick is to take an extremely limited view of both the ethical issue itself and of the general prevailing ethical attitudes that people seem to have towards helping the sick. This view would appear to be more Rawlsian than utilitarian since it asserts an ethical principle about 'fairness' that is not derived from maximising the sum total of satisfactions (whatever they are), but instead leans towards an egalitarian notion of 'equally available care for equally sick' or 'communism in health'.

Now here we have the basis for a much more satisfactory defence of the NHS-type structure, for if it is the case that this 'humanitarian spill-over' is as general as it would seem to be, then it becomes logical to devise an institutional form to enable effect to be given to this feeling. In particular, it implies divorcing access to care from payment and relating access instead to some universally applicable notion of the *need* for care. The attitude of the NHS defenders unfortunately obscured this clear implication, with the result that the definition of need was left untackled in any systematic way in the NHS, as was the related question of whose value judgements should be incorporated into such a definition.

A second major point missed by most participants in the controversy was that under *both* the NHS *and* insurance schemes, the individual consumer pays a price that is less than cost. In insurance schemes, indeed, without co-insurance terms (i.e., the insured person pays $x$ per cent of the cost and the insurance firm $100-x$ per cent) or deductibles (i.e. the insured person pays the first £$x$ of expense), the price of use to an insured person is zero — exactly as it is for the NHS patient, so we can except excess demand, queues and the introduction of additional rationing devices (or excessive total expenditure) under *either* system!

It is much to be regretted that most of the NHS defenders were socialists of the romantic variety who traditionally tend, in social questions, to associate hard-headedness with hard-heartedness and were hence antipathetic to a *rigorous* analysis of alternative institutions, for here they would have had a rather substantial point against the critics. However, they missed the point and so, again alas, they missed its corollary: that the issue must lie with the alternative supplementary rationing criteria that are used in a zero (or less-than-cost) user-price situation under either system. And here, surely, they would have had yet another solid point to make, for if the spill-over is of the sort we have described above and the community is a rather homogeneous one as regards values — as Britain would appear to be — then it follows that collective ownership by the State is a reasonably inferred means of ensuring that a single set of discriminating values is applied to the whole of the health delivery system. The point *was* however missed, and the job of rationing was left to the doctors who were neither socially qualified (by being socially accountable) nor professionally trained for it. Nor — and the poor doctors must be mighty thankful for this mercy — was there any mechanism for monitoring and correcting the interpretative decisions that they made.

Reviewing this argument in slightly more detail, the logic of the theory of spill-overs provides, it is generally agreed, a case for subsidising health care consumption (in those cases where health care constitutes the most effective method of giving comfort or of obtaining an improvement in health status, whether actual or, as with preventive programmes, potential). The spill-over argument, however, provides no generally received and clearly articulated case for public ownership of health care agencies such as the hospitals, as compared with a loosely thought out inference that, since there is a case for *some* government intervention (subsidies), then such intervention should be nothing less than *total* (subsidies *and* public ownership).

In practice, the options generally turn out to be between a system of not-for-profit publicly owned hospitals and system of not-for-profit private charitable hospitals such as characterises most hospitals in the USA and characterised the most famous hospitals in pre-NHS Britain.

Private charitable organisations such as hospitals have generally been formed to serve local communities and are financed principally out of funds supplied by those concerned with local problems. Sometimes the concern has been specific in a non-local way, as when trade unions or the Church operate a private charitable nursing home for the exclusive use of their own members or clergy, or where foundations are established for other minority groups (more commonly found among educational establishments). In all such organisations the trustees are responsible for the proper fulfilment of the objects of the charity in meeting the needs, as specified, of the beneficiaries, as specified.

In the case of the NHS, however, whose institutions are designed to fulfil objects that are national in their scope and which include a concern about a uniformly effective and efficient rate of activity throughout the community, it clearly becomes appropriate for the 'charity' to become a national one and, since the 'contributors' to this 'charity' are literally the taxpayers in the community, the inference seems very readily drawn that such institutions become publicly owned. In this sense the NHS can be viewed as a kind of national charity (Culyer, 1973, ch.7).

It is not unreasonable to ask whether there are any grounds for preferring the non-profit object to profit-making in health care provision. As it turns out, there is no need to invoke (as was so often done in the 'market-versus-the-State' debate) emotional slogans about 'profiteering out of sickness'. The basic argument against the profit motive in hospitals is, in so far as such organisations are successful at making profits — which in a generally competitive environment they would have to be in order to survive — that they could do so only to the extent that they satisfied their customers. Here we come to the nub of the argument and the essential fallacy in the position of the pro-market camp. Pursuing the useful analogy of the charity, the charity is not set up with the purpose of satisfying principally the wants of its beneficiaries, but those 'needs' of the beneficiaries that are chosen *by the benefactors*. To this end, the objects of all charities are clearly specified. The NHS, similarly, is to be seen as a setup to serve not the interests of its clients as they see them but such needs of such clients as its 'benefactors', viz. the whole community, choose to define. There is of course no reason generally to suppose that these needs will at all correspond to the demands of individuals or patients, regardless of how much they are subsidised by the State. Indeed, there is every reason to suppose that demands for 'ineffective' treatments or 'luxury' accommodation are in no sense relevant to any generally acceptable definition of need, or that the rationing criteria used by physicians in a profit-maximising institution would not correspond to the set of priorities chosen by those entrusted with the task of interpreting the community's wishes in this regard.

These arguments apply *a fortiori* in the more realistic case where the competitiveness of the market is not sufficient to ensure that proprietory hospitals actually do seek to maximise profits. Under competition, those who do so seek, but fail, will tend to disappear (e.g. by being 'taken over'); but under less rigorous — and more realistic — conditions, not only may hospitals fail to maximise profits but they may fail to be penalised by the market for so failing. In such an environment varying degrees of discretion exist for management to pursue courses of action that are not merely inconsistent with social priorities but even inconsistent with their owners' and their clients' preferences.

While it would certainly be possible to devise a complex subsidy system ensuring that only those receiving approved treatments would receive the subsidies and that subsidies would go only to those regarded as in greater need, it is clear even without a detailed working out of the administrative complexities that a publicly owned system providing approved régimes of care and allocating them according to approved criteria, *alongside* a system of private provision without subsidy, is a good deal more effective, *prima facie*, than this alternative.

If this argument is correct however it has a profoundly ironic implication. For, while it effectively refutes the case for a highly decentralised system, and in particular the pro-market case for privately owned hospitals (whether for profit or charitable) coupled with subsidies to patients, it also constitutes itself as a formidable attack on the NHS that the anti-market brigade were defending, because the NHS was never provided with the set of approved technologies and proper priorities (that is, the definition of 'need') that constitute, on this argument, its principal (indeed, its sole) justification.

From the 'market-versus-the-State' debate, then, has eventually emerged a remarkable insight — that the NHS is indeed a remarkably illogical institution — but for quite other reasons than those adduced by the critics. The real inconsistency of the NHS was that it represented a means without a specified end while for those ends which were specified it was either no means at all or else merely one of a number of plausible alternatives whose rival merits could not be settled by *a priori* debate.

But once we have established the ends of the NHS as meeting some clearly defined set of needs, its present form can be seen to be a suitable means only in its general form. In specifics it remains sadly lacking. In particular it still largely lacks, to this day, the definition of the needs and the institutional mechanisms within it to ensure that such needs are met as effectively and efficiently as possible.

While the 'market-versus-the-State' debate focused principally on the demand side of the problem and, as we have seen, failed to resolve by *a priori* means what were ultimately either empirical questions or inadequately comprehensive ethical questions, the real case for the NHS-type structure lies on the *supply side*. Health care is an area where, in principle, the effectiveness of techniques can be established by the scientific procedure of hypothesis formation and empirical testing (the objective being to try to falsify rather than verify). It is also an area where there is broad agreement about the meaning of effectiveness of treatment, and where measures of outcome can be devised. Historically, however, in all systems the medical professions have had enormous discretion both as to technique and as to allocation among the excessive number of claimants for their services that seems endemic in all systems too. That this is true even under the NHS is eloquent testimony to the incompetence of the demand-oriented approach, for not only does it fail to provide a satisfactory rationale for the public ownership of health institutions such as hospitals, but it has also led to the creation of no workable allocation criteria.

Such is the frailty of man's imagination in devising suitable social institutions that the very obverse of this inconsistency is to be found in the field of education. In education, the objectives are subtle and as varied as the individuals having an interest in it. The technology of education is likewise highly uncertain. Yet in this area we have seen monumental monotechnism ordered by the State (e.g. universal textbooks, standard examinations, universal comprehensivisation of schools) just where one would expect to see decentralisation of organisation, freedom of choice and the evolution of schools and universities of a fascinating variety as institutions respond to the enormous and profound differences in the expectations, religions and social attitudes of the clients and their families, with the State's role mainly the financial one of subsidising individual clients rather than institutions. The result has been disenchantment, truancy, alienation and, of course, interminable political controversy. Such could be the case only where a more or less homogeneous set of values relating to the ends of education and a dominant school of thought about the appropriate means is imposed upon a society containing many individuals in sympathy with neither point of view.

In health, where the British institutional form is in general — though quite by accident — arguably appropriate, we have scarcely begun to reap the potential benefits. While the task of identifying the effective means is one in which the social scientists' roles are probably restricted to the efficiency part of the exercise, the task of defining rationing criteria that correspond to meaningful notions of need is, while assuredly not uncontroversial, one where the social scientist has an extremely important role to play.

## BIBLIOGRAPHY

Arrow, K. J. (1963) 'Uncertainty and the Welfare Economics of Medical Care' *American Economic Review*, vol. 53
Buchanan, J. M. (1965) *The Inconsistencies of the National Health Service* London, Institute of Economic Affairs

Crew, M. (1969) 'Coinsurance and the Welfare Economics of Medical Care' *American Economic Review*, vol. 59

Culyer, A. J. (1971) 'Medical Care and the Economics of Giving', *Economica*, no. 151

Culyer, A. J. (1971) 'The Nature of the Commodity "Health Care" and its Efficient Allocation' *Oxford Economic Papers*, vol. 23

Culyer, A. J. (1972) 'The "Market" Versus the "State" in Medical Care' in McLachlan (ed.) *Problems and Progress in Medical Care* 7 Oxford University Press

Culyer, A. J. (1972) 'On the Relative Efficiency of the National Health Service' *Kyklos*, vol. 25

Culyer, A. J. (1973) *The Economics of Social Policy* London, Martin Robertson; New York, St Martins Press

Feldstein, M. S. (1963) 'Economic Analysis, Operational Research and the National Health Service' *Oxford Economic Papers*, vol. 15

Jewkes, J. and S. (1961) *The Genesis of the British National Health Service* Oxford, Basil Blackwell

Jewkes, J. and S. (1963) *Value for Money in Medicine* Oxford, Basil Blackwell

Klarman, H. E. (1965) *The Economics of Health* New York and London, Columbia University Press

Lees, D. S. (1960) 'The Economics of Health Services' *Lloyds Bank Review*, April

Lees, D. S. (1962) 'The Logic of the British National Health Service' *Journal of Law and Economics*, vol. 5

Lees, D. S. *et al.* (1964) *Monopoly or Choice in Health Services?* London, Institute of Economic Affairs

Lees, D. S. (1967) 'Efficiency in Government Spending – Social Services: health' *Public Finance*, vol. 22

Lees, D. S. and Rice, R. G. (1965) 'Uncertainty and the Welfare Economics of Medical Care' *American Economic Review*, vol. 55

Lerner, A. P. (1944) *The Economics of Control* London, Macmillan

Mushkin, S. J. (1958) 'Towards a Definition of Health Economics' *Public Health Reports*, vol. 73

Nichols, D., Smolensky, E. and Tideman, T. N. (1971) 'Discrimination by Waiting Time in Merit Goods' *American Economic Review*, vol. 63

Pauly, M. V. (1968) 'The Economics of Moral Hazard: Comment' *American Economic Review*, vol. 57

Rawls, J. (1972) *A Theory of Justice* Oxford University Press

Seldon, A. (1967) 'National or Personal Health Services', *Lancet* (i)

Smolensky, E., Tideman, T. N. and Nichols, D. (1972) 'Waiting Time as a Congestion Charge' in S. Mushkin (ed.) *Public Prices for Public Products* Washington DC, Urban Institute

Titmuss, R. M. (1963) 'Ethics and Economics of Medical Care' *Medical Care*, vol. 1 (reprinted as ch.21 in *Commitment to Welfare* London, Allen and Unwin, 1968)

Titmuss, R. M. (1967) *Choice and the Welfare State*, Fabian Tract 370, London, Fabian Society (reprinted as ch.12 in *Commitment to Welfare* London, Allen and Unwin, 1968)

# 8. Rationing Health Care Resources: the Second Step in Need Evaluation

Chapter 3 explored the effects of a number of factors on the demand for health and, hence, the demand for health care. In chapter 7 we have just seen the inconclusive nature of the results to be expected from operation on the money price of medical care. In this chapter we explore some ways in which, in the future, it may be possible for the NHS to fulfil its promise to meet health needs as and when they may occur. Because this task involves us finally in operationalising the notion of need we introduced in chapter 4 and have discussed throughout the book so far, it is helpful to restrict the sphere of application, but we shall not choose a trivial problem. Rather, we shall focus on the point at which the existence of excess demand in the NHS is most conspicuous: on the lists of those patients who are waiting for admission to hospital as in-patients.

The cost to a patient of receiving medical care in hospital can in general be conceived of having two main dimensions: a money cost and a time cost. In the NHS the money cost (unless one seeks an amenity bed as an NHS patient) is zero. The time cost varies with the length of in-patient stay and consequential convalescence at home or in another institution and is a cost to the extent that being there denies one the opportunity of engaging other valued work and/or non-work activities.

The 'problem' of waiting lists has conventionally been seen as a problem of demand and supply. In figure 8.1 the kind of analysis

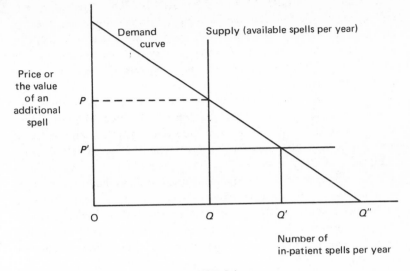

FIGURE 8.1

implicitly in mind is presented. The demand curve shows the values, in descending order, placed by all the relevant individuals in the community on in-patient spells of hospital treatment. At zero money price (OP'), OQ' spells are demanded. At a zero time price as well (e.g. with full compensation to patients of the opportunity cost of their time) OQ'' spells are demanded. Actually, at price OP' only OQ spells are actually available, so that in any time period there is an excess demand of QQ' — these spells must be either foregone entirely or else postponed (the patients put on a waiting list). That this is the kind of reasoning lying behind several people's thinking can easily be illustrated. For example, Arthur Seldon (1967) has written: 'if taxi fares and meters were (by analogy) abolished and a free National Taxi Service were financed by taxation, who would go by car, or bus, or walk? . . . the shortage of taxis would be endemic, rationing by rushing would be to the physically strong, and be more arbitrary than price, and the "taxi crisis" a subject of periodic public agitation and political debate.' A similar kind of reasoning lies behind an official 1963 Ministry of Health circular (HM(63)22), which gave guidance on waiting list management and emphasised that a long waiting list that is numerically stationary is not normally an indication of resource deficiency in any permanent sense: it represents instead a 'backlog' of cases which could (and should) be removed by determined short-term efforts including, for example, making additional operating theatres available temporarily, diverting beds from other specialties, reducing length of stay in hospital, performing surgery (e.g. on varicose veins) in out-patient departments and utilising hospitals maintained by the armed forces.

The 'solution' to the waiting list 'problem' implied by these two views is, however, different. The 'Seldon solution' would be to allow a money price to be introduced to ration out available supply to those with the highest valuations. In the short term, this would be $P'P$, giving a full price of $OP$. (To work effectively, it would need, as we have seen, to be accompanied by *no* insurance.) Presumably, in the longer term, as no additions to the list were made and the list fell in size, there would be some leftward shift of the demand curve until it settled in a new equilibrium where no postponed demands existed and the money price would be somewhat lower than $OP$ but higher than zero (i.e. $OP'$).

The 'HM(63)22 solution' is to cause the supply curve to shift out to the right using the means indicated above. Some of this would be a permanent shift since a permanent reduction in the length of in-patient stay permits a permanent increase in the throughput of patients. In the short term this would mean increasing capacity (and capacity utilisation) to a level at which a flow of spells in between $OQ'$ and $OQ''$ could be managed (it would be larger than $OQ'$ since a reduced length of stay would tend to reduce the time price of in-patient treatment and hence encourage demand). Again, however, presumably in the longer run, as the inherited stock of postponed admissions were run down, there would be some leftward movement of the demand curve until a new position was established, with a new equilibrium quantity probably somewhat lower than $OQ'$ but higher than $OQ$.

Unfortunately, this kind of analysis has three major deficiencies. First, the nature of the demand and supply of hospital care has one particular feature that falsifies most of the predictions of this analysis. Second, the principal concern of each school of thought has been with waiting lists rather than waiting times. Third, the concern has not so much been with meeting *needs*, which involves assessing the needs of those admitted as well as those possibly to be admitted, as with eliminating an excess *demand*, or 'shortage', in its behavioural sense. If we accept the view advanced in chapters 5 and 6 that it is the business of the NHS to meet needs if they can effectively be met (and the business of the private sector to meet any residual demands) then the focus must be wrong. Let us examine each of these points in turn before developing what seems to be a more appropriate approach to a solution of the *real* problem.

Although no one has experimented in the NHS with money prices for hospital surgery, attempts to interpret waiting list data as a proxy for excess demand for in-patient care have notably failed if judged by the consequences of supply changes. Both Feldstein (1964) and Culyer and Cullis (1975, 1976) failed to find what one would expect: that waiting lists would fall with increases in supply. Instead, as table 8.1 shows, waiting lists have remained remarkably stable. There are two principal reasons for this. On the one hand, since most of the supply increase has come about through a fall in the length of stay, this tends to generate an offsetting demand increase (owing to the fall in the time price of in-patient care — recall chapter 6). Much more important, however, is the fact that the demand for care is mediated by doctors whose perception of need, operationally and at the level of the individual patient, is what really decides whether a patient is admitted. Since doctors also control supply, the usually convenient separation of resource allocation problems into a demand side and a supply side (the two blades of Alfred Marshall's 'scissors') ceases to be valid, for the factors affecting one side can no longer be supposed to be independent of the factors affecting the other: a necessary prerequisite for the valid application of demand/supply analysis. Supply increases, therefore, instead of reducing the excess demand (as mediated by doctors), tend not only to enable the meeting of existing demands, but encourage GPs to refer more patients to hospital, and hospital doctors to assign more people to the waiting list, until a more or less 'conventional' waiting time is again reached.

In 1963 the Institute of Hospital Administrators (IHA) (1963) reported that many GPs did not send geriatric and surgical patients to hospital if they knew there was no chance of admission for a long time, while on the hospital side it is widespread practice not to put on the list all patients who may benefit. Generally, those listed are patients who will receive maximum benefit from treatment within, say, a period of six months to a year. (There are exceptions; a recent survey of 1971 waiting lists by the Department of Health and Social Security found that sometimes even cases considered by the consultant in charge to be urgent had been waiting for more than a year. But this was in a survey of hospitals where the 'problem' seemed particularly acute.) Thus, the

### TABLE 8.1

*Waiting lists, average length of stay, available beds and throughput capacity 1955–1971*

| YEAR | 1955 | 1956 | 1957 | 1958 | 1959 | 1960 | 1961 | 1962 |
|---|---|---|---|---|---|---|---|---|
| Total Waiting List (000's) | 444.0 | 420.6 | 430.3 | 433.3 | 466.2 | 454.2 | 435.4 | 462.9 |
| Total Waiting List per 1000 population | 10.0 | 9.4 | 9.6 | 9.6 | 10.3 | 9.9 | 10.1 | 9.9 |
| Average length of stay (days) | 22.9 | 22.2 | 21.6 | 21.0 | 20.1 | 19.5 | 18.5 | 18.1 |
| Available beds (000's) | 264.4 | 263.8 | 263.3 | 263.6 | 262.2 | 261.9 | 258.9 | 259.5 |
| Throughput capacity* | 11,546.6 | 11,883.1 | 12,190.2 | 12,552.9 | 13,042.6 | 13,429.8 | 13,995.1 | 14,335.6 |
| Waiting times† Mean (Weeks) | | | | | | | | 14.5 |

| YEAR | 1963 | 1964 | 1965 | 1966 | 1967 | 1968 | 1969 | 1970 | 1971 |
|---|---|---|---|---|---|---|---|---|---|
| Total Waiting List (000's) | 468.2 | 491.8 | 510.9 | 530.5 | 531.1 | 529.1 | 555.2 | 549.4 | 520.0 |
| Total Waiting List per 1000 population | 10.0 | 10.4 | 10.7 | 11.1 | 11.0 | 10.8 | 11.4 | 11.2 | 10.7 |
| Average length of stay (days) | 17.6 | 17.0 | 16.6 | 16.2 | 15.7 | 15.3 | 14.7 | 14.6 | 13.9 |
| Available beds (000's) | 260.0 | 259.4 | 259.6 | 259.3 | 260.3 | 260.2 | 259.8 | 257.5 | 257.8 |
| Throughput capacity* | 14,772.7 | 15,260.6 | 15,636.8 | 16,007.7 | 16,579.4 | 17,009.4 | 17,639.5 | 17,636.4 | 18,543.7 |
| Waiting times† Mean (Weeks) | 14.4 | 14.4 | 14.5 | 14.8 | 14.2 | 13.7 | 14.0 | 14.7 | 13.9 |

* Number of beds available divided by mean length of stay
† Excluding Maternity 1967–70

*Sources:* Forms SH3 summaries (DHSS *Hospital Costing Returns*);
DHSS *Report on the Hospital Inpatient Enquiry*, London, HMSO.

analysis tends to break down because decisions by doctors about a patient's claim on in-patient resources are not taken independently of the resources available — the more the resources, the more patients doctors will turn up to benefit from their utilisation!

Second, the focus on the 'problem' of lists has been misplaced. The problem is — or ought to be — to minimise not the list but the cost of waiting time. Yet it is the remarkable fact that since the inception of the NHS in 1948 there has been no survey of waiting patients to discover what costs (including inconvenience, work loss, costs to families and local authority services etc.) are imposed by the waiting system. Strictly, the problem should be to minimise the social costs (over time) of the average waiting patient multiplied by the size of the list — the importance of the latter depending entirely upon the size of the former.

The third deficiency of current conceptualisations of the rationing problem is the lack of systematic attention given to need. To the extent that need is taken into account, it is only clinical urgency that counts in the overwhelming majority of cases. Since most waiting patients are 'cold surgery' cases about which there is no great urgency, this is a plainly insufficient tool. In the IHA study of 82 hospitals in England and Wales and 10 in Scotland, to which reference has already been made, 46 hospitals reported that the person who authorised the placing of a name on the waiting list was the consultant concerned, while 39 stated it was either the consultant, Senior Hospital Medical Officer or the registrar. When asked whether there was any accepted medical criteria for inclusion on the waiting list 50 replied yes and 41 no. Stating that there was no accepted medical criterion for inclusion on the list, one hospital went on to say: 'Inclusion on the list is based on the assessment of the medical condition of the patient by the individual consultant in charge of the case. The medical criteria therefore vary according to the individual standards of each consultant although there would certainly be a level at which all consultants would agree that a case should be included on the waiting list.' In most hospitals the convention appears to be to classify the clinical urgency of the condition into three categories.

Several suggestions for improvement exist in the literature. The general line of thought is typified by Baderman et al. (1973): 'The consultant should assess priority on both clinical and social grounds and the degree of urgency should be clearly indicated on the waiting list.' More specifically, Luckman, McKenzie and Stringer (1969) argue that decision rules for admissions must be capable of taking into account the following characteristics for each patient:

>time already spent on the waiting list ($T$);
>
>urgency based upon the expected rate of deterioration of the patient's condition (e.g. suspected malignant neoplasms should come in quickly) ($W$);
>
>urgency based on the degree of disability (e.g. large hernias should come in more quickly than small ones) ($D$), and
>
>urgency based on social factors (e.g. wage-earners with many dependants should come in quickly) ($S$).

In this schema $W$, $D$ and $S$ are subjective assessments while $T$ is objective. These researchers proposed to combine the various factors into a priority index ($P$) as follows:

$$P = S^a DT^{Wb}. \tag{8.1}$$

A modification by Phoenix (1972) suggested combining $S$ and $D$ and setting $b = 0.5$ yielding the formula

$$P = DT^{\sqrt{W}}. \tag{8.1a}$$

An alternative formula has been proposed by Fordyce and Phillips (1970). Using similar characteristics ($T$, $W$, $D$ and $S$), they proposed the formula

$$P = (aS)(bD)(T)c^W \tag{8.2}$$

and, additionally, suggested that $a = b = 1$ and $c = 2.2$.

A third formula is that of the London Hospital (n.d.), which takes the form:

$$P = \frac{c^W(T + 28)}{\sqrt{L}} \tag{8.3}$$

where $L$ is expected length of stay.

One feature of the formulae is that the exponents attached imply that, for those variables, the index score increases at a faster rate than the measured variable itself — implying not only that the worse a patient's state was in any one respect the higher his priority number, but also that his priority number would rise faster than the degree of severity in that one respect. This seems to be a plausibly desirable characteristic. A second feature is that variables with exponents (or variables used as exponents) will not 'trade off' with other variables at a

constant rate. This too seems highly plausible and a desirable feature of
an admissions index. These points can be illustrated in a diagram that
will by now be becoming familiar to the reader. Consider formula (8.2)
as it applies to patients having the same degree of social need for care
and having waited the same time. Given the assumptions made by
Fordyce and Phillips, the formula becomes

$$P = D(2.2^W). \qquad (8.2b)$$

$D$ and $W$ are two measures of urgency, it will be recalled. Let us imagine
them, for the moment, measured on a scale of $1-5$ in ascending order
of severity. For all possible scores on $D$ and $W$, the value of the index
(ignoring the effects of $S$ and $T$) would be those in figure 8.2. The
qualities described above can now be readily seen. A doubling of the
scores of $D$ *and* $W$ (say, from 1,1 to 2,2) leads to a more than doubling
of the index score $P$ (from 2.2 to 9.6 in this case). To make the second

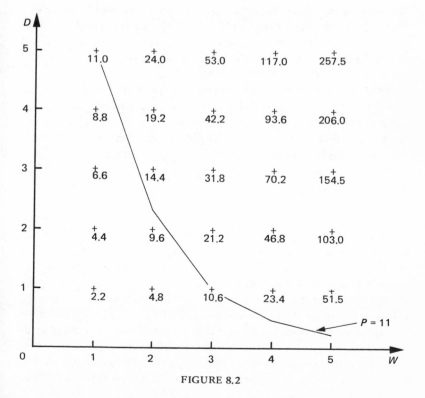

FIGURE 8.2

feature clear, imagine that $D$ is perfectly divisible. We then calculate all those values of $W$ and $D$ yielding the same index score — in the matrix this has been done for $P = 11$. The concavity (from above) of the line joining all these points illustrates the second principle — as a patient scores less on one measure of urgency, it requires increasing degrees of urgency on the other measure to give him the same priority.

While each of these features is likely to be regarded as a desirable characteristic of any formula of need (especially the second, rather subtle, feature), it is important to see their implications in an actual decision-making context. First, it is *not* necessary to interpret patient A (with $D = 2$, $W = 1$) as having twice the priority of patient B (with $D = 1$, $W = 1$). But he will clearly have higher priority and should be admitted before patient B. Second, *two* patients with ($D = 1$, $W = 1$) will *collectively* have the same priority as one with ($D = 2$, $W = 1$). Thus, if the costs of care for the two patients are less than those for the one patient, it is tempting to infer that there is more to be gained from admitting them earlier. We return to this interesting possibility below. Third, some patients having widely differing characteristics will have the same index score and, hence, equal priority. Thus, in our illustration, patient C with ($D = 5$, $W = 1$) will have approximately the same priority as D with ($D = 1$, $W = 3$).

We close this stage of the discussion by emphasising what is probably now quite clear (see above, chapter 4): that the selection of variables for inclusion in the index and the weights attached to them are *policy* decisions embodying particular value judgements. They are not matters that can be decided by social science (or any other kind), nor are they matters, in a *national* health service, that should be decided by persons without public accountability.

We turn now to the question of which variables to include. Although, as has been stated above, the selection and the precise weights to be attached are a matter for policy-makers, one is able to say something (i) at the level of principle about which variables should *not* be included, and (ii) about the likely candidates for inclusion without actually imposing our own value judgements.

As will be clear from the earlier discussion, it is important to separate the *need* for in-patient care from its supply. Ultimately, of course, need and the resources available for meeting it must be brought together in order to decide which needs are to be met (and when). Confusion, however, is encouraged if need and supply are brought together too soon. This leads us to object to formulae (8.1a), (8.1b) and (8.2) as indexes of priority – rather, they are indexes of need. Formula (8.3), however, incorporating length of stay (which has nothing whatever to do with a patient's need for care), can be interpreted as an indicator of priority (though the method of introducing $L$ can be questioned).

The characteristics that are the most likely candidates for inclusion in an index are as follows:

(i) time already spent on the waiting list $(T)$;
(ii) urgency based on the expected rate of deterioration of the patient's condition $(C)$;
(iii) urgency based on the patient's health status $(H)$;
(iv) urgency based upon the 'social productivity' of the patient and the number of economic dependants $(E)$;
(v) urgency based upon other social factors $(S)$.

Before indicating the kind of measurement that is appropriate for these variables, it is as well to specify more clearly the differences between $C$ and $H$, and $E$ and $S$. The urgency based upon the expected rate of deterioration of the patient's condition $(C)$ is intended as a purely clinical judgement about prognosis, relating to a choice concerning the optimal point of intervention. Urgency based upon the patient's health status $(H)$ relates to the patient's ability to function in society in an effective and trouble-free way. A person suffering much pain and unable to work would, on this criterion, get higher priority than one who was not.

Developing indicators of $E$ and $S$ is much harder, and the principal reason for this is that we are in substantial ignorance about the actual financial and social costs borne by waiting patients and those who are also affected by their waiting. This is partly, of course, the consequence of the present lack of systematic consideration given to these questions as a routine matter in the hospital services.

The notion of productivity referred to in $E$ should not be a narrow concept – for example, the contribution to GNP – and it should also take account of the extent to which waiting does or does not impair the patient's productive capacity. Impairments to his comfort are included in $H$. In practice, the kind of complication that a refined concept of productivity would introduce into the index can be avoided, as will be seen, by devising rather simple characterisations of this type of urgency.

Of the various components of the index, only time spent waiting is directly measurable in ready units that can fairly easily be picked out from the records. The others require some scoring procedures such as those suggested by Luckman *et al.* (1969); Rosser and Watts (1972) or in chapter 4 above. The following paragraphs indicate the kind of thing that could be possible.

Urgency can be scaled in a variety of ways. Consider the simplest form, using a three-point scale. In such a system there is maximum likelihood that different observers would assign the same numbers in any given case, as it is only when the variables become more finely divided that the possibility of differing judgements about urgency becomes a serious problem.

Urgency based on clinical deterioration may be scaled (following Luckman *et al.*, (1969) as:

$C = 1$,   no significant deterioration if left untreated in the immediate future;

$C = 2$,   noticeable deterioration if left untreated in the immediate future;

$C = 3$,   rapid and substantial deterioration if not urgently treated.

Urgency based on health status may be scaled as:

$H = 1$,   suffering only minor pain for which analgesics such as aspirin might be prescribed and/or minor disability including the ability to do all except possibly the heaviest housework, and to work with no more than a slight impairment of normal effectiveness;

$H = 2$,   suffering moderate pain (e.g. equivalent to severe headaches) and/or moderate mental distress, and/or being restricted only to light housework or having work performance severely limited, with the prospect of a marked improvement with treatment;

$H = 3$,   suffering very severe pain and/or severe mental distress, and/or being unable to do any housework, go to school or to work; being confined to bed or unconscious, with the prospect of a marked improvement with treatment.

Urgency based on social productivity may be scaled as:

$E = 1$,   no economic loss to the family unit owing to condition;

$E = 2$,   substantial economic loss to the family unit owing to the condition, or complete dependence upon social security benefits, but no economic dependants;

$E = 3$,   family unit with economic dependants completely dependent upon social security benefits because of the condition, or suffering a very large economic loss.

Finally, urgency based upon other social factors may be scaled as:

$S = 1$,  no social disadvantages (e.g. adequate home circumstances for coping with an invalid; no likely emotional strain to be imposed upon family members);

$S = 2$,  postponement of admission likely to impose substantial pressure on household's ability to cope with the patient;

$S = 3$,  severe social hardship would be caused by a failure to admit early. (Since children are often regarded as worthy of priority attention, their cases could be scaled only over $S = 2$, $S = 3$.)

Several points are worth emphasising about the verbal descriptions attaching to the scores. First, they should describe a set of circumstances that are readily understandable by the person assigning the scores and that are also readily separable one from the other to maximise their reproducibility by different persons. Second, the circumstances should be ascribed clearly to the condition. For example, an unemployable person who has a big hernia would not normally receive $E = 3$. Third, the circumstances described in the score must be capable of being altered by the procedures for which a patient would be admitted to hospital. Luckman *et al.* argued for a completely prognostic approach to the $H$ component, where each score describes the probability of a small, significant or major improvement in health status, and this too is built into our proposal, though in a slightly different form which places greater emphasis on the patient's current state. Fourth, it will be noted that the $E$ component contains an implicitly relativist view of economic hardship, with, for example, the very well-off who suffer a large fall in income being given equivalence with the not-so-well-off who fall to dependence on social security benefits. This is plainly a matter of value judgements. Perhaps a large loss to the well-off would be regarded as equivalent to a smaller loss for the less well-off — provided, of course, that the large loss were large enough!

It should also be noted that the measures should be those appropriate at the first possible point of admission. For example, where patients are called up, say, a month ahead of the proposed date of admission, those assigning the scores should bear this in mind. In hospital departments such as orthopaedics, where emergency admissions are frequent and a short notice list is also kept to help even out the patient flow, the index can also be used to select from among those patients who are willing to come in at short notice.

It will also be apparent that the assigning of the scores, once a workable system has been established, need not be a job exclusively falling on the shoulders of senior medical personnel. While it would doubtless be desirable that they should rank patients according to $C$, and that $H$ should normally be ranked by someone who has familiarity with the clinical diagnosis in question, the other variables require no very special expertise (and could be ranked by a secretary) provided, of course, that the overall index score does not lead to perverse results in the view of the consultants. Moreover, to retain awareness of 'human control', it is always possible to have the admitting officer select from among the top (say) $1.5N$ patients, where $N$ is the number to be admitted. This flexibility would also permit an appropriate selection of patients to make up a theatre list and, in teaching hospitals, to select cases that would be suitable for teaching purposes.

How is one to effect a reconciliation of the use of the admissions index, based on the notion of need and incorporating considerations of fairness, in the context of the efficiency requirements discussed in chapter 5? If, as was suggested above, the index is used merely as a ranking of the patients' needs for admission, it will serve as a method of discriminating between patients' claims on existing hospital in-patient resources, and, provided that each department's beds are as fully utilised as it is efficient for them to be, then the outcome will probably be an improvement in efficiency in the short term — that is, during the period in which the resources available to each department are taken as fixed.

If, however, the objective is selected, as it may well be, of reducing to the greatest extent possible the total needs of waiting patients, then it is desirable — indeed necessary — to attribute a stronger interpretation to the index by focusing on the actual index scores themselves rather than their relative positions. The reason for this is plain: a patient (with a needs index number) is admitted only at the cost of not admitting (now) another patient (also with an index number). If lengths of stay differ between conditions (as they usually do), and if the needs of persons differ as between conditions (as they normally will), then the clear possibility arises that a greater reduction in total need is possible if, say, two persons with relatively short expected lengths of in-patient stay and low index scores are admitted instead of one person with a long expected stay and a high index score. This is plainly the rationale behind the London Hospital Index.

The desire for short-term efficiency — maximum reduction in need out of given resources — therefore suggests that patients be admitted in such a way as to maximise the daily reduction in the total index of all waiting patients. Ignoring the fact that increased turnover tends to reduce average bed occupancy, the inference to be drawn is that an appropriate admissions index is thus a needs index divided by expected length of stay. Patients with high scores in terms of need who were excluded by this procedure would have a higher probability of admission in the time period immediately following. Indeed, by a suitable choice of form for the formula, this probability can be made as high as the policy-maker wishes (by, for example, using time (days or weeks waiting) as an exponent on the urgency characteristics).

This procedure implies that the admissions index is calculated for each waiting patient as a matter of routine each time period (say, weekly) as it will apply at the next possible date of admission and the list is worked down in descending order of admission priority (viz. need index divided by stay) until the department in question has a full complement of in-patients.

In principle, there is no reason why the admissions index should not be used in conjunction with a booking system (as well as a short notice list) whose great advantage is that patient uncertainty about the time of admission is minimised and whose minor advantage is that waiting lists, as such, need no longer be kept (though waiting times would, of course, remain a reality).

In the longer run, the needs index could be used to improve the balance between departments, hospitals and regions. In principle, maximum efficiency then obtains when the marginal need in each department, hospital and region is the same. In a society where one patient is to be regarded as equally important as any other (save for the characteristics in the needs index) this would also fulfil the objective of fairness — it would be impossible to reduce needs in one area without increasing them in a second by *more* than they had been reduced in the first area.

It has been suggested from time to time that the relative length of waiting lists could be used as a method of planning the balance of resources as between various hospital specialties. This is a most dangerous interpretation of waiting list data. For example, since 95.6 per cent of waiting patients in 1974 were in surgical specialties (including gynaecology) — a proportion that has been steadily increasing (91.2 per cent in 1956) — this interpretation would suggest that surgical specialties should be expanded compared with, say, medical specialties. Such a view ignores (among other things) the important fact that the nature of the overwhelming majority of medical cases is that delayed admission is likely to have very marked deleterious effects on the patient's condition – in short, that such patients would, in any case, achieve high scores if the admissions index were to be applied to them.

The correct view, as has been argued above, is to focus less on the size of the list and more on the needs of those patients who are on it. This implies an expansion of surgical specialties (not a reduction in medical specialties) when the costs of an expanded service are 'worth' incurring to reduce the needs that they would be able to effect. This in turn implies either an implicit or an explicit (which is much to be preferred) exercise of the sort described below.

To ascertain the optimal size of in-patient facilities it is necessary to attach some social value (a policy matter) to the admissions index. The optimum would be reached when the additional cost of providing more in-patient resources (or costs saved by reducing them) equalled the social value attached to the reduction (or increase) in the need for in-patient care. Thus, if $V$ represents the social value (in £) of a one-unit reduction in the needs index ($\Delta N$), global efficiency exists when

$$\Delta \text{cost} = V \Delta N$$

(where $\Delta$ indicates an increment or decrement), provided, of course, that marginal needs are everywhere equalised.

Inherent in this discussion has been the view that the efficient and fair operation of the health service requires the establishment of *national norms* and a substantial reduction in the discretion of individual hospital doctors. Their task would remain, at the individual level, to make judgements about the numbers to be assigned to the individual characteristics of individual patients. But they would do this in the context of a nationally promulgated needs formula, with its coefficients representing nationally promulgated value judgements, and the local conditions as regards lengths of in-patient stay. And that is surely not inappropriate in a *national* health service!

This chapter, then, has completed the discussion of chapter 4 and has shown how the concept of need there developed may be applied in an entirely different context from those sketched in chapter 4. It has also show how the idea of need can be developed to enable discrimination among individuals, according to need, and how it has to be modified by resource considerations (in this example, length of stay being used as a rough guide to resource demands) if the goal of maximum need reduction with given resource endowments is to be attained. Finally, looking much further ahead into the future, we have explored the process of valuing needs reduction that *must* (explicitly or implicitly) be gone through in decisions concerning net investment in health care resources, rather than redeployment of existing resources.

The innocuous looking formula, $\Delta cost = V\Delta N$, on page 110 is the tersest possible statement of what every social and humanitarian cost—benefit exercise seeks to accomplish. While to date some success has been achieved in measuring $\Delta cost$, the right-hand side of the equation poses the real problems. The emphasis in this book has been, of course, on measures of $N$ (and hence $\Delta N$). The estimation of $V$ raises again all the problems concerning value judgements that we met in chapter 4. Much of what goes to make up $V$ will probably never be quantifiable by the experts. It is an area where the judgement of publicly accountable persons rules supreme, for statements about the social value of reductions in need are, *par excellence*, statements about health service policy at the highest plane. It is here that the crucial elements of compassion and humanitarianism come starkly in; here that charges against the NHS, or claims for it, that it is either an inhumane, uncaring bureaucracy or the triumph of social responsibility over selfishness, are ultimately tested. This is the ultimately irreducible element where uncompromising moral choices have to be made by someone. Their task will, however, have been eased to the extent that what can be quantified has been quantified and what lower-level value judgements may properly be made have been made. By clarification of the issues, by a narrowing down of the grey areas, by eliminating as far as is humanly possible all that is not inherently imponderable, the act of faith we are making says that we shall begin to approach the fulfilment of the objectives of the NHS. And it *is* an act of faith — one cannot *prove* that less ignorance of the facts of ill health and medical efficacy and more explicit analysis of the issues of choice lead to better policy. But in view of the alternatives, one *has* to believe that they do.

## BIBLIOGRAPHY

Baderman, H. *et al.* (1973) *Admission of Patients to Hospital* London, King Edward's Hospital Fund
Culyer, A. J. and Cullis, J. G. (1975) 'Hospital Waiting Lists and the Supply and Demand of Inpatient Care' *Social and Economic Administration* vol. 9

Culyer, A. J. and Cullis, J. G. (1976) 'Some Economics of Hospital Waiting Lists in the NHS' *Journal of Social Policy*, vol. 4

Feldstein, M. S. (1964) 'Hospital Planning and the Demand for Care' *Bulletin of the Oxford University Bulletin of Statistics*

Fordyce, A. J. W. and Phillips, R. (1970) 'Waiting List Management by Computer' *The Hospital*, vol. 66

Institute of Hospital Administrators (1963) *Hospital Waiting Lists — A Report of the Study and Research Committee of the IHA*

London Hospital (n.d.) 'Selection from an Orthopaedic Waiting List', unpublished.

Luckman, J., McKenzie, M. and Stringer, J. C. (1969) *Management Policies for Large Ward Units* Institute of Operational Research, Health Report No. 1

Ministry of Health (1963) *Reduction of Waiting Lists, Surgical and General*, HM(63)22

Phoenix, C. J. (1972) 'Waiting List Management and Admission Scheduling' in M. Abrams (ed.) *Spectrum 1971: A Conference on Medical Computing* London, Butterworth

Rosser, R. and Watts, V. C. (1972) 'The Measurement of Hospital Output' *International Journal of Epidemiology*, vol. 3

Seldon, A. (1967) 'National or Personal Health Services', *Lancet* (i)

# 9. Regional Patterns

The ideal of equal available care for equal need could never have been implemented in the first twenty or so years of the NHS's existence for the simple reason that 'need' had never been given operational (or even meaningful!) content, nor was there much attempt to do so. But the principle of availability was firmly established in the catechism of the health service. The 1946 NHS Bill aimed to create a system of health services 'available to everyone regardless of financial means, age, sex, employment or vocation, area of residence or insurance qualification'. In view of this it was all the more remarkable that the first attempt systematically to examine the regional availabilities of NHS resources was made as late as 1970 — and even then in a report commissioned by a body not famous for its commitment to the enshrined ideals of the NHS. The data in the new General Household Survey will in the not too distant future, it is to be hoped, enable similar systematic analysis of availability (and utilisation) by social class.

The finding by Cooper and Culyer (1970, 1972), however, that systematic and apparently uncompensated variations in provision were persisting (and in some cases increasing) has resulted in greater attention being paid to the question of territorial justice in health care provision and in official attempts to rectify imbalances. The problems involved in these efforts are the subject of this chapter.

Table 9.1 shows the variation by region (in the pre-reorganised NHS) of revenue expenditures *per capita*. Later we shall see even bigger variations at the more local level of the new area health authorities.

TABLE 9.1.

*Revenue expenditure* per capita *by region, 1971—72*

| Region | Hospital services | | Community health services | | | | | |
|---|---|---|---|---|---|---|---|---|
| | | | Local authority | | GP services | | Total | |
| | £ | % of mean | £ | % of mean | £ | % of mean | £ | % of mean |
| SW Metropolitan | 33.58 | 141 | 3.92 | 117 | 10.56 | 110 | 48.06 | 130 |
| NW Metropolitan | 31.89 | 134 | 3.76 | 112 | 10.80 | 112 | 46.44 | 126 |
| SE Metropolitan | 26.44 | 111 | 3.55 | 106 | 10.23 | 106 | 40.23 | 109 |
| NE Metropolitan | 26.27 | 110 | 3.56 | 106 | 8.60 | 89 | 38.43 | 104 |
| Liverpool | 25.47 | 107 | 3.22 | 96 | 9.68 | 101 | 38.36 | 104 |
| South Western | 22.96 | 96 | 3.28 | 98 | 10.22 | 106 | 36.47 | 99 |
| Leeds | 22.91 | 96 | 3.08 | 92 | 9.29 | 97 | 35.28 | 96 |
| Newcastle | 21.80 | 91 | 3.36 | 100 | 9.40 | 98 | 34.56 | 94 |
| Manchester | 21.63 | 91 | 3.36 | 100 | 9.48 | 99 | 34.48 | 94 |
| Oxford | 21.41 | 90 | 3.45 | 103 | 9.32 | 97 | 34.18 | 93 |
| Wessex | 20.58 | 86 | 3.06 | 91 | 10.04 | 104 | 33.69 | 91 |
| Birmingham | 20.28 | 85 | 3.15 | 94 | 8.91 | 93 | 32.34 | 88 |
| East Anglia | 19.66 | 82 | 2.91 | 87 | 9.45 | 98 | 32.01 | 87 |
| Sheffield | 18.44 | 77 | 3.08 | 92 | 8.95 | 93 | 30.47 | 83 |
| Mean | 23.87 | | 3.35 | | 9.61 | | 36.83 | |
| Coefficient of variation | 18.8% | | 8.1% | | 6.1% | | 14.2% | |
| Max. as % of min. | 140.1% | | 117.1% | | 112.4% | | 130.5% | |
| Min. as % of max. | 54.9% | | 74.2% | | 79.6% | | 63.4% | |

*Source:* Noyce *et al.* (1974)

The table reveals a substantial variation in expenditures per head (Sheffield, for example, receiving 77 per cent of the average and the S.W. Metropolitan Region 141 per cent of the average).

In the 1970 Cooper and Culyer study, thirty-one indexes of provision were constructed from official sources and in almost every instance Sheffield appeared 'worse off' than Oxford. Moreover, the indexes were usually correlated with one another so that a region performing badly according to one criterion did badly also according to another. At specific resource measurement level, the general impression conveyed by expenditure data was confirmed. Newcastle had twice as many gynaecologists per head of female population as Sheffield; Birmingham had twice as many consultants as Sheffield; Liverpool twice as many psychiatrists as Manchester.

There has been no thorough study of trends in inequalities since the inception of the NHS. Over the five years studied by Cooper and Culyer, relative inequalities seemed to be increasing both in terms of hospital and GP services. *Per capita* expenditure in 1971–72 was, however, slightly less unequal overall than in 1950–51 (Cooper, 1975).

The general pattern in the early 1960s was, it would appear, in proportionate terms not so very different (as far as the hospital services are concerned) from what it was after the First World War. Since the inception of the NHS, there has been some attempt, both by direct control and financial inducement, to control the distribution of GPs; but hospital financing methods had the prewar distribution of resources built into them until very recently and since the number of hospitals has grown by only 3 per cent since the war this growth could not be expected to have much impact on inequality.

That the perpetuation of the prewar resource distribution was built into the hospital system can be seen by the description of the financing method in the Guilleband Report (Ministry of Health, 1956):

(T)he total amount available is first divided between the Regional Hospital Boards as a whole and the Boards of Governors [of teaching hospitals] as a whole, broadly in proportion to the expenditure of these two groups in the last year for which actual figures are available. The Regional Boards' share is then divided among the individual Boards, leaving aside a limited amount for the running costs of new developments. The sum is available for the maintenance of existing services, the allocation being on the basis of permitted increases to support the increased costs of existing services, with a report and consultation procedure to ensure that the final total equals the sum available.

More recent detailed data relating to area health authorities (AHAs) before reorganisation and based on the area profiles the shadow authorities prepared have been analysed by Buxton and Klein (1975) and relate to 1971–72. Their main results are summarised in table 9.2 and show the percentage variation from the mean in spending and bed provision in forty-nine area health authorities.

The numbers speak for themselves, of course, and the large array of minuses in, say, the Trent AHA confirms the general impression that earlier data have given about the Sheffield region (though the data indicate that Sheffield itself is relatively well endowed). The total range of *per capita* spending is from +62 per cent in Liverpool to −69 per cent in Sandwell.

Before turning to an examination of what is, and what might be, done about this remarkable situation in a health care system that has

TABLE 9.2

Variations in hospital spending by area, 1971–72

| | Population (thousands) | Current expenditure | % Variation from National Average for Provision per Capita | | | | | | | | | |
| --- | --- | --- | --- | --- | --- | --- | --- | --- | --- | --- | --- | --- |
| | | | BEDS | | | | | | | | | |
| | | | Total | General medicine | General surgery | Traumatic and orthopaedic surgery | Mental handicap | Mental illness | Maternity | Maternity (adjusted)† | Geriatric and chronic sick | Geriatric and chronic sick (adjusted)‡ |
| *Mersey* | | | | | | | | | | | | |
| Cheshire | 865 | −11 | 39 | −25 | 0 | 28 | 77 | 122 | −17 | −18 | 42 | 65 |
| Liverpool* | 607 | 62 | 38 | 192 | 130 | 90 | −47 | −69 | 99 | 105 | 31 | 36 |
| St. Helens and Knowsley | 377 | −34 | 13 | 5 | −25 | −12 | −100 | 165 | −43 | −44 | −60 | −55 |
| Sefton | 425 | −15 | −6 | 71 | 23 | −1 | 19 | −90 | −12 | −10 | −18 | −19 |
| Wirral | 355 | −10 | −2 | 60 | 85 | 95 | −86 | −77 | 17 | 21 | −23 | −40 |
| *Oxford* | | | | | | | | | | | | |
| Berkshire | 624 | −10 | 1 | −11 | 1 | 7 | 49 | −37 | 27 | 20 | −19 | 1 |
| Buckinghamshire | 477 | −29 | −24 | −29 | −33 | −54 | −54 | −39 | 9 | 5 | −23 | −9 |
| Northamptonshire | 468 | −32 | −15 | −36 | −9 | 17 | −59 | −24 | −9 | −8 | 49 | 53 |
| Oxfordshire* | 505 | 3 | 24 | −21 | −19 | 60 | 71 | 43 | 6 | 2 | −19 | −5 |
| *South Western* | | | | | | | | | | | | |
| Avon* | 901 | 14 | 23 | 33 | −7 | 32 | 190 | −42 | 36 | 37 | −5 | −9 |
| Cornwall | 378 | −30 | −7 | −38 | −41 | −30 | −39 | 31 | −5 | 4 | 24 | −6 |
| Devon | 896 | −14 | 14 | −32 | 0 | −18 | 46 | 18 | 6 | 18 | 24 | −11 |
| Gloucestershire | 467 | −36 | −18 | −45 | −22 | 5 | −100 | 4 | 18 | 21 | 10 | 9 |
| Somerset | 386 | −17 | 21 | −44 | −38 | −40 | 29 | 77 | 17 | 26 | 66 | 40 |
| *South West Thames* | | | | | | | | | | | | |
| Croydon | 334 | N.A. | 35 | N.A. | N.A. | N.A. | 331 | 4 | 0 | N.A. | 0 | 5 |
| Kingston and Richmond | 250 | N.A. | 30 | N.A. | N.A. | N.A. | −13 | 170 | −9 | N.A. | −38 | −44 |
| Merton, Sutton and Wandsworth* | 680 | N.A. | 58 | N.A. | N.A. | N.A. | 40 | 105 | 26 | N.A. | 29 | 17 |
| Surrey | 1111 | N.A. | 32 | N.A. | N.A. | N.A. | 124 | 86 | 4 | N.A. | −23 | −20 |
| West Sussex | 627 | N.A. | −19 | N.A. | N.A. | N.A. | −28 | 11 | 1 | N.A. | −34 | −56 |

| | | | | | | | | | | | |
|---|---|---|---|---|---|---|---|---|---|---|---|
| *Trent* | | | | | | | | | | | |
| Barnsley | 225 | -51 | -55 | -22 | -29 | -31 | -100 | -88 | -8 | -7 | -29 | -20 |
| Derbyshire | 885 | -37 | -31 | -63 | -45 | -39 | -45 | -21 | -29 | -28 | -12 | -9 |
| Doncaster | 280 | -18 | -15 | -29 | -7 | -14 | 69 | -64 | 56 | 54 | -12 | 7 |
| Leicestershire* | 798 | -40 | -27 | -63 | -31 | -58 | -13 | -26 | -9 | -10 | -15 | -8 |
| Lincolnshire | 503 | -14 | 16 | -36 | -6 | -8 | 58 | 35 | 2 | 5 | -1 | -5 |
| Nottinghamshire* | 973 | -17 | -23 | -28 | -10 | 4 | -53 | -31 | -21 | -21 | -15 | -5 |
| Rotherham | 243 | -62 | -60 | -57 | -39 | -65 | -100 | -100 | -33 | -34 | -5 | 16 |
| Sheffield* | 572 | 34 | 20 | 12 | 22 | 43 | 19 | -2 | 32 | 38 | 34 | 32 |
| *Wessex* | | | | | | | | | | | |
| Dorset | 554 | -18 | 10 | N.A. | N.A. | N.A. | -39 | 63 | -5 | 8 | 36 | -12 |
| Hampshire* | 1353 | -21 | -4 | N.A. | N.A. | N.A. | -13 | 46 | -15 | -17 | -25 | -22 |
| Isle of Wight | 110 | -12 | 6 | N.A. | N.A. | N.A. | -14 | 52 | -18 | -28 | 19 | -24 |
| Wiltshire | 676 | -10 | 5 | N.A. | N.A. | N.A. | -26 | 4 | 9 | 10 | 56 | 53 |
| *West Midlands* | | | | | | | | | | | |
| Birmingham* | 1098 | 10 | 4 | 2 | 8 | 34 | -28 | 0 | 14 | 20 | 20 | 25 |
| Coventry | 337 | -30 | -44 | -24 | -24 | 21 | -100 | -95 | 8 | 7 | -25 | -3 |
| Dudley | 294 | -40 | -40 | 18 | 22 | -9 | -56 | -86 | -18 | -22 | -33 | -19 |
| Hereford and Worcester | 559 | -12 | 46 | -28 | -13 | -20 | 68 | 61 | -7 | -8 | 16 | 20 |
| Sandwell | 330 | -69 | -74 | -57 | -51 | -60 | -100 | -100 | -49 | -47 | -55 | -49 |
| Shropshire | 337 | -22 | -3 | -43 | 9 | 155 | -95 | -3 | -1 | -1 | 51 | 54 |
| Solihull | 192 | 20 | 74 | -2 | 22 | -38 | 292 | 21 | 114 | 96 | -30 | 8 |
| Staffordshire | 962 | N.A. | 3 | -35 | -28 | -5 | -33 | 51 | -17 | -21 | 31 | 61 |
| Walsall | 273 | -50 | -10 | -45 | -8 | -63 | 296 | -100 | -28 | -31 | -41 | -17 |
| Warwickshire | 456 | N.A. | 9 | -10 | -6 | -18 | 133 | -8 | -6 | -11 | 23 | 54 |
| Wolverhampton | 268 | N.A. | -37 | -38 | -12 | -50 | -100 | -78 | 25 | N.A. | -32 | N.A. |
| *Yorkshire* | | | | | | | | | | | |
| Bradford | 461 | -13 | 10 | 18 | 3 | -22 | -11 | -31 | 48 | 54 | 23 | 21 |
| Calderdale | 195 | -33 | -21 | -5 | -5 | -12 | -10 | 88 | 31 | 41 | 59 | 44 |
| Humberside | 838 | -25 | -7 | -39 | -15 | -14 | -12 | -26 | 4 | 6 | 11 | 17 |
| Kirklees | 369 | -13 | 15 | N.A. | N.A. | N.A. | -86 | 95 | 56 | 63 | 55 | 51 |
| Leeds* | 737 | 2 | 0 | 4 | -16 | 20 | -15 | -8 | -15 | -18 | 0 | -1 |
| N. Yorkshire | 628 | -15 | 21 | -6 | 3 | 22 | 3 | 10 | 8 | 11 | 66 | 55 |
| Wakefield | 302 | 1 | 49 | 21 | 31 | 96 | 27 | 109 | -3 | 11 | 38 | 51 |

*Teaching Area.

†Beds per female in age group 15–44.

‡Beds per person in age group 65 and over.

N.A. = Not available from profile.

*Source:* Buxton and Klein (1975).

been 'socialised' for over twenty-five years, let us turn briefly to the major problem of interpretation — whether or not the variations may correspond to any variations in need. There are, of course, also other problems of interpretation and some of the more important of these will be discussed in the context of methods of procuring a more equitable distribution.

Unfortunately, there is at present no way of relating the regional data on morbidity in the General Household Survey to levels of service provision in the NHS. However, a fairly recent attempt to relate community health expenditure, hospital revenue expenditure and hospital capital expenditure to some crude indicators of social and health status were reported in Noyce *et al.* (1974). Their results are shown in table 9.3 and are by no means heartening: higher birth rates are associated with lower *per capita* expenditure of all three kinds; there is no significant relationship between mortality rates and spending; there is a negative (but not highly significant) relation between infant mortality and all three kinds of spendings, and a strong positive association between social class and spending.

The rather depressing picture is thus one of quite substantial *per capita* variations, no systematic relationship of provision with measured

TABLE 9.3.

*Correlations between health and social status indicators and health service spending*

|  | Community health expenditure | Hospital revenue expenditure | Hospital capital expenditure |
|---|---|---|---|
| Birth rate | −0.6388 | −0.5242 | −0.0580 |
| Death rate | 0.2420 | 0.0324 | −0.3318 |
| % population over 65 | 0.3600 | 0.1227 | −0.1268 |
| Infant mortality rate | −0.4458 | −0.3305 | −0.2626 |
| % of population managerial and professional | 0.8307 | 0.7937 | 0.4700 |
| % of population semi-skilled and unskilled manual | −0.7455 | 0.7822 | −0.2314 |

Note: Coefficients >0.78 are significant at 0.1% level, >0.6614 at 1% level, and >0.5325 at 5% level.

Source: Noyce *et al.* (1974), p. 556.

need (and sometimes a perverse apparent relationship) and no apparent trend in the long term for any improvement.

In 1971—72, as a result of political awareness that a 'problem' really did exist, the Department of Health and Society Security introduced a formula for the allocation of current account budgets to regional hospital board hospitals. This formula incorporates:

(i) *population*: the forecasted population of the region, after allowing for expected interregional patient flows (which have not been included in previously reported *per capita* provision data);

(ii) *beds*: the national average expenditure on beds and out-patient attendances multiplied by the daily number of occupied beds and number of out-patient attendances (by specialty);

(iii) *case-flow*: the number of in-patient and out-patient cases in the region (by specialty) multiplied by national average expenditure.

Each element is then incorporated into a formula designed to 'normalise' regional budgets over time. Thus, the population element takes the proportion of expected regional population of total population and allocates, on this element, the same proportion of the total available allocation. The bed stock element takes the regional bed stock and multiplies it by national average expenditure per bed (allowing for case mix variation) to gain the regional entitlement on this element. The case flow element takes the regional case flow and by multiplying it by the national average expenditure per case derives the regional entitlement on this element. Naturally, inflation is allowed for. Since each element tends to produce a different entitlement for the region, the actual entitlement is a weighted sum of all three, with population having a weight of 0.5 and the other two a weight of 0.25 each.

An arithmetical simplified example of the way the formula works is given in West (1973). Suppose the following are the relevant basic data:

1. National total budget for hospitals — £1,000m.
2. National population — 50m.
3. National average cost per bed — £3,000
4. National average cost per case — £100
5. Previous period's regional hospital allocation — £150m.
6. Regional population — 5m.
7. Regional bed stock — 40,000
8. Regional case flow — 1.1m.

Allocation on population grounds = (6)/(2) × (1)
= £100m.
Previous allocation = £150m.
Therefore population based adjustment = −£50m.

Allocation on bed stock grounds = (7) × (3)
= £120m.
Previous allocation = £150m.
Therefore bed-based adjustment = −£30m.

Allocation on case flow grounds = (8) × (4)
= £110m.
Previous allocation = £150m.
Therefore case flow-based adjustment = −£40m.

Total allocation = ½ population entitlement =   50m.
+ ¼ bed stock entitlement   =   £30m.
+ ¼ case flow entitlement   =   27.5m.
= £107.5m.

Total adjustment = ½ population adjustment = −£25m.
+ ¼ bed stock adjustment   =   −£7.5m.
+ ¼ case flow adjustment   =   −£10m.
= −£42.5m.

Since the formula might have a severe impact if introduced suddenly, it was planned to take effect over the ten years 1971–72 to 1981–82, with only 10 per cent of the adjustment made in year one, viz. in our example £4.25m. rather than £42.5m. In addition, where new hospital building has taken place a special allowance under the 'Revenue Consequences of Capital Schemes' system of supplementation is to be continued until 1978.

Clearly, the application of any formula such as this raises a large number of important questions into which it would not be appropriate to go in this present book (a useful and detailed discussion is to be found in Rickard, 1974). For our purposes, three questions regarding any such formula-finance are paramount. These concern, first, the effects it is likely to have on hospital behaviour, secondly, the extent to which it really does produce a matching of availability with need and, thirdly, whether it is likely to do so in a fair way. In the remainder of the chapter we shall examine the present formula with reference to each of these criteria in turn.

Making guesses about hospitals' reactions to changes in the parameters (whether financial, or otherwise) is one of the least developed parts of hospital economics. However, one general approach has been found quite generally applicable to non-profit organisations, among which we must of course include NHS hospitals, and this is that such organisations, at the very least, seek to maximise their budgets at any level of activity. The reasons are not hard to seek: the higher the budget, the more finance there is for the administrators and doctors to purchase resources that *they* regard as desirable (whether these are socially desired by those who ultimately are the 'owners' of the hospital, i.e. the public, is, of course, another matter). Now while this statement is far from being a complete description of the aims of, say, the doctors (some of whom like a quiet life, while others want power over large staffs, prestige, professional recognition and advancement, still others wish to serve their patients devotedly, to do research or to build up their private practices and probably most want to do more than one or these things) and is, moreover, an inadequate basis for a rigorous analysis of hospital behaviour, it is suggestive and seems to accord with experience (was any doctor ever *overpaid*, was any hospital ever *over*-financed according to that doctor or hospital?).

If so, then in addition to the rather obvious fact that the formula tends still to award more, because of the bed stock element, to those with high bed stocks, and hence to retain the historic inequalities, hospitals seeking higher budgets (viz. all hospitals!) have an incentive to reduce expenditure per case and hence, out of a given budget, to increase the case flow. While this may, on the face of it, seem desirable and efficient it is by no means so clearly desirable or efficient on closer examination.

For one thing, efficiency in the hospital service requires the production of any given level or type of service at a specified quality (defined with respect to the outcome — with all its relevant dimensions, clinical and non-clinical, individual and public — not the inputs) *at least cost*, not *at least expenditure*. Thus, if case flow is increased by too-early discharge, causing additional real costs in the community health service and the household sector, and possibly re-admission to hospital later (so that what might have been one case now appears in the statistics as two, or three, or . . . .), then it is by no means clear that the cause of efficiency in health care is being served.

Secondly, quality of care may be reduced — but the fact that the patient is less satisfied with his hospital food (if such a thing were possible!) or was more likely to die or suffer from iatrogenic disease (i.e. disease induced by medical practice) or be disabled in any one of a variety of ways upon discharge is not in the formula and would not penalise the hospital, whereas cutting down in any of these ways — provided that it increases case flow — would positively benefit the hospital. The professions are placed in the embarrassing position of being invited to trade off professional standards of care and cure against the institution's financial advantage.

Our second head for general consideration of revenue allocation budgets relates to the matching of resources to needs. It is quite clear that the population element in the present formula is an extremely crude proxy for need. At the present time, however, we know that rather little can be done about this. For the future, our analysis suggests that there are two potentially fruitful lines of inquiry. The first is the more obvious and direct one of actually measuring health status in an appropriate way for this purpose (see the discussion in chapter 4) and of devising priorities (chapter 8). The second is more indirect and flows from our discussion of the demand for health in chapter 3. We know that those with a low demand for health are those who have the lowest health status index. We may presume that those with the lowest health status are also most likely to be in need — though such a view must be qualified (i) by our requirement that the NHS attempt only to meet needs for which technically effective and cost-effective procedures exist, and (ii) by a process of social evaluation that is not to be expected to view all kinds of ill health as equally important. Finally, we also know from analyses that have been made of the demand for health function that it is particularly affected by a definable set of variables, some of which at least may be easier to measure than need itself and which may, therefore, be able to serve as the basis for the construction of a surrogate measure of need. Note that we are *not* proposing to derive this surrogate from the demand function *for health care*, for we retain a sharp distinction between demand and need. But it could be derived from the demand *for health* function, and the various weights that would have to be attached to the various components would reflect the social process (an important part of which consists in selecting those whose responsibility this choice problem will be) of evaluating the need. (Beware of 'experts' who recommend or use their own sets of weights — whether they know it or not they are assuming the mantle of God.)

The major determinants (other than price) of the demand for care

are: age, sex, earned income, marital status and education. In addition, environmental hazards to health such as industrial and occupational structure, pollution etc., and other related indicators such as neonatal deaths and the number of handicapped and impaired persons, may prove to be valuable supplements.

In principle, then, it is possible to imagine an index being compiled for the representative individual in an area or region and *then* applying the population element.

Indeed, with either the direct or the indirect method, no other element than the (adjusted) population element would be required in the formula, save to effect a smooth transition from the *status quo*. Indeed, in a variation of the formula likely to be introduced in the not-too-distant future, the population element's weight is likely to be substantially increased.

Finally, we have the general head of fairness to consider. It will be clear enough from the discussion above that the case flow and bed stock elements in the present formula do not of themselves promote equality or fairness in provision – indeed, the case flow element can promote greater inequalities as they have traditionally been measured (West, 1973). More generally, and supposing that we have derived an acceptable (if crude) indicator of area or regional needs, an interesting dilemma in the efficiency/equity conflict may arise.

If the objective were, out of the limited resources available, to minimise the amount of unmet need (which seems a very reasonable objective), then we already know from chapter 8 that we cannot do this with a given budget without knowing the cost of eliminating a 'unit' of need (assuming – which is a basically egalitarian assumption – that a given reduction in ill health is of equal value whomsoever and wheresoever an individual experiencing it is). The reason is that some needs are more costly to eliminate by a given quantity than others are, and it would clearly be foolish, given the objective stated, to eliminate some need by spending the whole budget on needs that are relatively costly to eliminate, when more need could have been removed by spending the same budget on those that are less costly to remove.

This gives rise to a dilemma. It is unfortunately the case that many of those who are in need do not demand health care, even when it is available. In order to meet such need, therefore, additional efforts are required (health education, publicity, screening campaigns, etc.) which raise the cost of meeting need – and where such low demanders are a high proportion of the population, the unit cost of reducing need in such an area will (other things equal) be higher than in other areas where the proportion of low demanders is lower. Thus, a policy of minimising need, which seems superficially attractive, may (at least to some readers) appear less attractive when the implication is appreciated: that some areas may, in such circumstances, be left with a higher level of unmet need than others. This, of course, is merely a specific example of a perfectly general proposition, that *whatever* the source of the higher unit cost of reducing need, lower cost needs will be reduced first, until the entire budget is spent.

An alternative objective is to equalise the amount of residual unmet need in all areas. This may seem attractive, until its corollary too is appreciated: that by redeploying resources more need could in total be reduced! In short, an egalitarian approach to the meeting of need in a world where resources are limited actually implies inflicting unnecessary pain, distress and ill health on people! That may seem a remarkable conclusion to have reached, but it is an inescapable one — and there is absolutely no prospect that health care resources are ever going to be unlimited!

This is an appropriate moment to return to the beginning of this chapter, for while we may with some substantial confidence assert that the objective of equal availability is not being met, and if we are prepared to make an additional value judgement in favouring equal residual needs in each area we may also assert with some confidence that this objective is not being met, we *cannot* assert that the objective of maximum reduction of need is *not* being met, merely by observing the inequalities, for since the cost of care varies from region to region (the true social cost as well as NHS expenditure costs) so will provision and so will residual needs where maximum reduction is being attained. Of course, there are lots of reasons for believing that the maximum reduction is *not* being achieved. But if you believe, like the author does, that the only really moral policy for the NHS is to minimise, out of a given budget, the amount of unmet need in society, it is somewhat disquieting, to say the least, to discover that provision inequalities are inherent in the just and moral solution!

# BIBLIOGRAPHY

Buxton, M. J. and Klein, R. E. (1975) 'Distribution of hospital provision: policy themes and resource variations' *British Medical Journal*, 8 February

Consumers' Association (1975) 'NHS: How well does it work?' *Which?*, August

Cooper, M. H. (1975) *Rationing Health Care* London, Croom Helm (ch. 7)

Cooper, M. H. and Culyer, A. J. (1970) 'An economic analysis of some aspects of the NHS' in I. Jones (ed.) *Health Services Financing* London, BMA

Cooper, M. H. and Culyer, A. J. (1972) 'Equality in the NHS: Intentions, performance and problems in evaluation' in M. M. Hauser (ed.) *The Economics of Medical Care* London, Allen and Unwin

Cooper, M. H. and Culyer, A. J. (1972) 'An economic survey of the nature and intent of the British NHS' *Social Science and Medicine*, vol. 5

Department of Health and Social Security (various) *Hospital Costing Returns* London, HMSO

Department of Health and Social Security (1974) *Health and Personal Social Services Statistics for England* London, HMSO

Department of Health and Social Security and Office of Population Censuses and Surveys (various) *Report on the Hospital Inpatient Enquiry* London, HMSO

Griffiths, D. A. T. (1971) 'Inequalities and management in the national health service' *The Hospital*, vol. 67

Maynard, A. K. and Tingle, R. (1974) 'The mental health services: a review of the statistical sources and a critical assessment of their usefulness' *British Journal of Psychiatry*, April

Maynard, A. K. and Tingle, R. (1975) 'The objectives and performance of the mental health services in England and Wales in the 1960's' *Journal of Social Policy*, vol. 4

Ministry of Health (1956) *Report of the Committee of Enquiry into the Cost of the National Health Service* (the Guilleband Report), Cmnd. 9663, London, HMSO

Noyce, J., Snaith, A. H. and Trickey, A. J. (1974) 'Regional variations in the allocation of financial resources to the community health services' *The Lancet*, 30 March

Office of Population Censuses and Surveys (1973) *The General Household Survey, Introductory Report* London, HMSO

Political and Economic Planning (1944) *Medical Care for Citizens* London, PEP

Rickard, J. H. (1974) *The Allocation of Revenue Expenditure Between Areas in the Reorganised Health Service* Oxford, Department of the Regius Professor of Medicine

Spicer, C. C. and Lipworth, L. (1966) *Regional and Social Factors in Infant Mortality* London, HMSO or General Register Office, Studies on Medicine and Population Subjects

Townsend, P. (1974) 'Inequality and the health service' *The Lancet*, 15 June

West, P. A. (1973) 'Allocation and equity in the Public Sector: the hospital revenue allocation formula' *Applied Economics*, vol. 5

# 10.  International Comparisons

This chapter can do no more than provide an outline of comparisons between countries. After a broad comparison between EEC countries, North America, Japan and the USSR, measuring in crude terms health and some factors affecting the demand for health, the focus will be upon administrative arrangements in three countries, where the systems differ in a striking way: the UK, West Germany and Canada.

Table 10.1 gives a sample of recent data relating to health status (which are subject, of course, to all the limitations noted in chapter 4) together with a few environmental variables that are known (see chapter 3) to affect the demand for health. Given the paucity of systematic empirical inquiry about the demand for health at the national level, let alone at the international level, such information is useful (apart from its use as self-congratulatory material – when appropriate) more for the questions it poses than for the lessons it implies. To answer each and any of these questions (e.g., what role do speed limits and drunken driving legislation play in explaining the difference between British and Belgian road fatalities?) itself requires a degree of model specification and testing that is very rare. Moreover, the statistics can be extremely misleading. For example, the mortality rate from appendicitis in 1966 in England and Wales was 0.9 per 100,000 population compared with, say, 3.3 in West Germany and 0.6 in Canada. More detailed examination shows, however, that of the German cases only one-quarter proved, after a pathologist had examined a sample of the removed appendices, to have had acute appendicitis (Lichtner and Pflanz, 1971). Clearly, some patients are

TABLE 10.1.
*Comparative health in selected countries*

| | Infant mortality per 1,000 live births, 1972 | Expectation of life at birth, 1967 | | Death rates per 100,000 population by selected cause, 1971 | | | | | | | | Maternal deaths per 100,000 live births, 1969 | Road deaths per 100,000 population, 1972 | Vehicles per 100 population | Average number of years of schooling | Alcohol consumption: litres per head per year, 1969 | Tobacco consumption: lbs per adult per year, 1970 |
| | | | | Infective and parasitic | | Malignant neoplasms | | Cardiovascular disease | | Accidents, poisonings, violence | | | | | | | |
| | | Male | Female | Male | Female | Male | Female | Male | Female | Male | Female | | | | | | |
|---|---|---|---|---|---|---|---|---|---|---|---|---|---|---|---|---|---|
| UK | 17.6 | 69.0(c) | 75.3 | 9 | 6 | 264 | 214 | 608 | 602 | 55 | 40 | 19.4(c) | 14(f) | 30(f) | 11.0(f) | 6.2 | 5.9 |
| Belgium | 20.5(a) | 67.9 | 74.3 | 16 | 9 | 276 | 210 | 561 | 517 | 107 | 65 | 20.5 | 32 | 31 | 11.3 | 6.7 | 7.5 |
| Denmark | 13.5(b) | 70.6 | 75.4 | 7 | 6 | 244 | 220 | 538 | 435 | 95 | 56 | 16.8 | 22 | 33 | 10.2 | 6.4 | 8.1 |
| France | 16.0(a) | 68.6 | 76.0 | 18 | 12 | 245 | 180 | 378 | 417 | 121 | 71 | 24.9 | 35 | 42 | 10.1 | 17.7 | 5.8 |
| West Germany | 22.5 | 67.7 | 73.9 | 16 | 8 | 247 | 228 | 538 | 550 | 111 | 64 | 53.1 | 31 | 31 | 9.3 | 11.4 | 6.7 |
| Irish Republic | 17.7 | 69.0 | 73.4 | 14 | 9 | 207 | 174 | 581 | 514 | 64 | 36 | 31.8 | 21 | 20 | 9.8 | 5.9 | 6.5 |
| Italy | 27.0(a) | 68.4 | 74.0 | 20 | 12 | 214 | 156 | 434 | 451 | 78 | 33 | 60.6 | 22 | 32 | 7.9 | 14.1 | 3.9 |
| Luxembourg | 13.5(a) | 66.3 | 72.7 | 11 | 7 | 314 | 190 | 641 | 573 | 120 | 63 | – | – | – | – | 8.7 | – |
| Netherlands | 11.4(a) | 71.3 | 76.0 | 7 | 7 | 225 | 165 | 406 | 343 | 70 | 43 | 19.4 | 24 | 42 | 9.7 | 5.1 | 8.9 |
| Canada | 17.1 | 68.8 | 75.2 | 6 | 5 | 161 | 127 | 410 | 311 | 100 | 42 | – | 29 | 44 | 11.0 | – | – |
| Japan | 11.7 | 70.5(d) | 75.9(d) | 26 | 15 | 133 | 102 | 291 | 255 | 83 | 35 | 24.5 | – | – | 11.1 | – | 9.4 |
| USA | 18.5(a) | 67.4(d) | 75.2(d) | 10 | 7 | 179 | 142 | 567 | 455 | 114 | 45 | 24.5 | 26 | 53 | 12.3 | 5.9 | – |
| USSR | 24.3(b) | 65.0(e) | 74.0(e) | – | – | – | – | – | – | – | – | 32.0 | – | – | – | 2.2(g) | – |

(a) provisional
(b) 1971
(c) England and Wales
(d) 1972
(e) 1968–69
(f) Great Britain
(g) 1968, beer and wine only

*Sources: Social Trends* no. 5 (1974); Maxwell (1974); *Demographic Yearbook* (1973)

dying not of the disease but from the procedures adopted after the (wrong) diagnosis! (recall chapter 5). Cause of death is subject to interpretation for other reasons too. British rates for pneumonia seem relatively high. But many old persons who die of this disease (the 'old man's friend') often suffer from one or more other chronic diseases, and precisely to which cause death is ascribed is subject to international variation. For these reasons, the categories in table 10.1 have been drawn deliberately broadly (but even then they may mislead).

Table 10.2 displays the results of the most recent attempts to compare spending on health at the international level. The absolute percentages of GNP are to be interpreted with caution because of the difficulties found in settling a common international definition of health care expenditure and of adjusting official data to accord with this definition. Probably more reliable – and certainly of more policy concern – is the increasing share taken by health care in recent years. Unfortunately, however, little is known about the reasons for this. A general pervading factor is that the demand for health care rises with incomes as we saw in chapter 3. However, this is insufficient to account for the differences between the countries shown in table 10.2. Partly,

TABLE 10.2.
*Health care expenditures*

| | As % GNP | | | | Average annual growth rate of health expenditure at constant prices (SSA) |
|---|---|---|---|---|---|
| | 1961 (Abel-Smith) | 1968 (OHE) | 1969 (SSA) | 1972 (Maynard) | |
| UK | 4.2 | 4.69 | 4.8 | 5.1 | 1962–69     5.6 |
| France | 4.4[b] | 4.90[c] | 5.7 | 5.5[d] | 1963–69     10.9 |
| West Germany | 4.5[a] | – | 5.7 | 5.8 | 1961–69     6.8 |
| Netherlands | 4.8[b] | – | 5.9 | 6.7 | 1963–69     10.1 |
| Canada | 6.0 | 7.25 | 7.3 | – | 1961–69     10.1 |
| USA | 5.8 | 6.71 | 6.8 | – | 1962–69     6.9 |
| Sweden | 5.4 | 6.26[c] | 6.7 | – | 1962–69     9.2 |

[a]estimate by US Social Security Administration
[b]1963
[c]1967
[d]1971

*Sources*: table 24 in Abel-Smith (1967); table 1 in OHE (1970); tables 1 and 2 in Simanis (1973); table 3, p. 257 in Maynard (1975).

however, real supply factors are also at work: policy decisions about length of stay in hospital and the impact of changing technology; a shift towards relatively more complex diagnostic and therapeutic procedures in the 1960s after the relative prominence of drug treatment; changing balances between institutional and community care; changes in finance (particularly in the USA with the introduction of the two federal health insurance programmes known as Medicare and Medicaid) and the existence of administrative structures in countries that may or may not have a restraining, or its converse, effect. In each country each of these factors has, in different measure, been present, and collectively they have operated against the common background that health care is a relatively labour-intensive industry with well organised professional associations and trade unions. There is also a widely differing prevalence of countervailing powers (including competition in the market) to hold down monopoly rents and the indulgence by the professions in costly — but dubiously efficient — chrome-plated technological extravagance (monotechnism again).

Table 10.3 provides some illustrative data about the resources on which these additional expenditures have been spent. The picture (limited though it is) suggests in general an increasing real input of manpower with decreasing emphasis on hospital bed provision and shortening lengths of in-patient stay. The differences at any one point in time between the countries are, however, extremely striking and suggest very strongly, as do all these patterns, that medical technology and the clinical view of 'need' are not the absolute things so frequently asserted but are indeed as we have argued them to be throughout this book.

The extraordinary thing about table 10.3 is that we have very little knowledge about whether the general trend of increasing expenditure on health care has been accompanied by any increase in health in any of the communities or whether, more reasonably, aggregate health status in each country would have been any lower without the increase or with a smaller increase. Nor, at the comparative level, do we know whether the *institutional* procedures adopted in one country are more productive of health than the procedures adopted in another.

An answer to the question about the effects of different institutional forms cannot be found by looking at the facts — scarce though they are. In order to relate institutional form to results we need a theory of *behaviour* that enables us to link the actions of patients, doctors, administrators and politicians to the environment in which they live. From such a theory expectations or predictions about behaviour

## TABLE 10.3.
### Health care resources, 1960–70

| | Physicians per 10,000 population | | Dentists per 10,000 population | | Nurses per 10,000 population | | Psychiatric hospital beds per 10,000 population | | All hospital beds per 10,000 population | | Average length of in-patient stay (days) | |
|---|---|---|---|---|---|---|---|---|---|---|---|---|
| | 1960 | 1970 | 1960 | 1970 | 1960 | 1969 | 1960 | 1969 | 1960 | 1969 | 1965 | 1969 |
| England and Wales | 10.5 | 12.3 | 2.5 | 2.7 | 17.8 | 31.7 | 46.5 | 38.3 | 104.7 | 95.4 | 12.7 | 11.1 |
| Belgium | 12.8(a) | 15.4(a) | 1.5 | 1.9 | – | 10.2(b) | – | 26.4(b) | 79.9 | 79.8(b) | 13.1 | 14.6(b) |
| Denmark | 12.3 | 14.4 | 5.0 | 7.0 | 37.7 | 47.2 | 21.0 | 22.5(b) | 104.4(d) | 91.6(b) | 14.5 | 13.4(b) |
| France | 10.0 | 13.2 | 3.5 | 4.3 | 18.6 | 25.8 | 19.5(d) | 21.9 | 145.3(d) | 100.0 | 20.0 | 18.0 |
| West Germany | 14.9 | 17.2 | 5.7 | 5.1 | 22.0 | 22.1 | 17.3 | 18.9 | 104.6 | 111.4 | 20.0 | 18.5 |
| Irish Republic | 10.5 | 10.7 | 2.1 | 2.1 | – | 37.2(c) | 72.8 | 57.0 | 213.0 | 128.0 | 15.8 | 15.0 |
| Italy | 15.9(a) | 18.1(a) | – | – | 7.6 | 6.5 | – | 21.6 | 89.1 | 105.4 | 14.8 | 13.4 |
| Luxemburg | 9.7 | 10.6 | 3.8 | 3.1 | 13.2 | 23.2 | 37.9 | 40.7 | 123.8 | 116.9 | 14.7 | 14.4 |
| Netherlands | 11.2 | 12.5 | 2.2 | 2.5 | – | 44.8 | 24.7(d) | 32.2(b) | 79.2(d) | 96.9(b) | 18.6 | 17.9 |
| USA | 13.4 | 15.8 | 5.6 | 5.0 | 27.9 | 33.5 | 43.7 | 30.3 | 91.8 | 81.2 | 8.6 | 9.3 |
| USSR | 18.0 | 23.8 | 1.4 | 3.8 | 27.8 | 39.7 | – | 9.7(e) | 81.1 | 106.7 | – | – |

(a)includes those practising dentistry
(b)1968
(c)1971
(d)1959
(e)1967

Source: Maxwell (1974)

differences are formed which the facts may suggest to be more or less plausible interpretations of causal processes. While some progress has been made of this sort, it remains unfortunately the case that empirical studies of behaviour in the health care industry are precious few, for this is an arena where the proponents of alternative institutions (especially the ideological proponents in Britain — see chapter 6) have preferred abstraction and have been extremely *ad hoc* in their treatment of the facts. A nice illustration of this propensity is to be found in the following bit of academic history. In 1964 the American economist Burton Weisbrod (Weisbrod, 1964) introduced a new element to the problem of determining the ideal capacity of hospitals by pointing out that available capacity, even if not used, was of social value because *people value the options* it opens up and which higher capacity utilisation forecloses (i.e. it is nice to know now, even though you are well, that *if* you fall sick there will be a high probability of early admission to hospital). According to this argument, it follows, unless special arrangements are made in the market, that market-oriented systems like that in the USA would tend to over-utilise capacity relative to public benefit systems like the NHS where, at least in theory, the spill-overs are supposed to be accounted for in hospital planning. (At the time, average occupancy was about 77% in both the USA and the NHS). About the same time, Richard Titmuss in England, who rarely had anything good to say about health care in the United States, argued that occupancy was higher in Britain and that this was, moreover, a Good Thing because it indicated the relative efficiency of the NHS (Titmuss, 1968). Dennis Lees, Titmuss's main opponent, who rarely had anything good to say about the NHS, adduced evidence showing that, in fact, the American hospitals had the higher occupancy and, thus, unwittingly, supported Weisbrod's prediction about the relative disadvantage of the market system while rebutting Titmuss's argument about its disadvantages (Lees *et al.*, 1964). Since in this argument the British participants did not share the same view about what the facts were, it is scarcely surprising that they did not share the same theory about behaviour or definitions of concepts.

The three countries selected for more detailed comparisons at the administrative level are the UK, Germany and Canada (in inverse order or their *per capita* income). Each is a developed country and each has in the course of the last decade made substantial changes in its system of organising health care. Each appears also to have set itself the same broad objectives in health care (a fully comprehensive and accessible service), and so may be compared, perhaps, with greater legitimacy than, say, the UK and the USA. While the problems confronting each are often the same, differences do arise that seem to be fairly clearly attributable to their administrative differences.

## I THE NATIONAL HEALTH SERVICE

Governmental health insurance was first introduced by the National Insurance Act 1911 (Part I) which was modelled after the German sickness insurance scheme introduced there in 1883. The Act covered workers earning less than £160 per year – about 13 million at the time – and made available sickness benefits in cash and GP medical care. The existing non-profit organisations such as Friendly Societies, which had previously provided insurance on a private basis, were used to collect flat rate premiums from the worker (fourpence), the employer (threepence) and the State (twopence) and to pay out benefits. GPs wishing to join the scheme built up a 'panel' of patients and were paid, in most areas, a capitation fee. The patient paid nothing to his doctor, nor did he pay for drugs on prescription. Although coverage in terms of both the income limit (and the inclusion of dependents) and benefits was extended in the period leading up to the Second World War it had become clear by then that a more comprehensive approach, and one that fully incorporated the hospitals, was desirable.

Hospitals were managed either under the Poor Law (until 1935) or were private charities – the Voluntary Hospitals. These latter supplied most of the beds and the prestigious institutions were among their number. They also developed their own insurance schemes for hospitalisation (10 million beneficiaries by 1937) but suffered increasingly from cash flow problems. At both the GP and the hospital level, marked differences in local resource availability grew up. On the one hand, the insurance system was such that, given inflexibility of premiums, approved societies sought to choose the least risky members, and in any case health levels varied widely across the country, so that some societies ran substantial surpluses and extended their benefits while others could barely make ends meet. On the other hand, the siting of the Voluntary Hospitals was dependent upon the initiative of locally charitable and wealthy persons, which meant that the poor of London had relatively abundant hospital facilities but the poor in most areas had only the Poor Law – or ex-Poor Law – institution.

The particular form of the new arrangements finally emerged in 1948. Medical care coverage was complete and for the entire resident population. The NHS had three branches: hospital and specialist services; local authority services such as home helps, ambulances, and midwifery; and local executive councils controlling GP, dental, ophthalmic and pharmacy services. The private hospitals were (almost entirely) taken over by the State and organised under fifteen regional hospital boards (RHBs) in England and Wales. Teaching hospitals retained, under boards of governors, an independence from regional or local bureaucracy. Below the RHBs were 330 hospital management committees at the local level in England and Wales.

Relative expenditure by these three basic divisions of the pre-1974 NHS are shown in table 10.4, which indicates the enormous preponderance of hospital expenditures and the increasing shares taken by the hospitals and local authorities.

Table 10.5 shows the sources of finance of the NHS. A popular myth in Britain has it that the NHS is financed from national insurance contributions. In fact, the NHS part of the insurance contribution has never accounted for more than about 14 per cent of total expenditure and the bulk of this finance is, of course, found from general, not earmarked, taxes.

The NHS was reorganised in 1974. From then on England and Wales had a single administrative structure encompassing hospital, GP and most of the community health services formerly provided by local authorities. Health services in Scotland and Northern Ireland were also reorganised along basically similar lines. The central authority remains the Department of Health and Social Security headed by the Secretary of State for Social Services, with responsibilities for Scotland, Wales and Northern Ireland lying with those regions' respective Secretaries of State.

In England fourteen regional health authorities (RHAs – the reorganisation is to be particularly noted for its production of a welter of acronyms) form area plans in conformity with national policy guidelines and allocate finance to the lower tier area health authorities (AHAs) whose responsibilities are to provide comprehensive health services in their areas, which coincide with those of the local authorities. There are ninety AHAs. AHAs are further subdivided into 205 districts, each with a district management team (DMT). The DMT's task is to manage and coordinate local services, decide priorities and needs.

The fundamental idea behind the reorganisation was to introduce

TABLE 10.4.

NHS expenditure by type, 1950–72 (selected years) in percentages*

| Year | Hospital services | Pharmaceutical services | General medical services | General dental services | General opthalmic services | Local authority health services | Other† | Total |
|---|---|---|---|---|---|---|---|---|
| 1950 | 54.9 | 8.4 | 11.7 | 9.9 | 5.2 | 7.8 | 2.0 | 100 |
| 1955 | 57.3 | 9.6 | 10.2 | 6.3 | 2.5 | 8.7 | 5.4 | 100 |
| 1960 | 56.4 | 10.1 | 9.8 | 6.3 | 1.9 | 9.0 | 6.5 | 100 |
| 1965 | 60.5 | 11.1 | 7.8 | 5.1 | 1.6 | 10.2 | 3.7 | 100 |
| 1967 | 59.9 | 10.6 | 7.9 | 5.0 | 1.4 | 10.7 | 4.5 | 100 |
| ‡1969 | 61.2 | 10.1 | 7.8 | 4.7 | 1.4 | 10.4 | 4.5 | 100 |
|  | (63.1) | (10.4) | (8.0) | (4.8) | (1.5) | (7.4) | (4.8) |  |
| 1970 | 64.2 | 10.0 | 8.3 | 4.9 | 1.4 | 7.0 | 4.4 | 100 |
| 1971 | 65.5 | 9.8 | 8.1 | 4.8 | 1.3 | 6.9 | 3.6 | 100 |
| 1972 | 66.0 | 9.7 | 7.9 | 4.5 | 1.2 | 6.8 | 3.9 | 100 |

*Local and central government expenditure (capital and current) and consumer payments.

†Includes grants, central administration and such items as research and laboratory costs not falling on any one service.

‡A new definition of NHS expenditure is used after 1969 owing to the creation of local authority social service departments.

Source: Office of Health Economics The Cost of the NHS London, OHE, 1974.

TABLE 10.5.

*National health and welfare services: sources of finance in Great Britain*

| Source | Unit | 1958–59 | 1965–66 | 1968–69 | 1969–70 | 1970–71 | 1971–72 |
|---|---|---|---|---|---|---|---|
| All services | £ million | 803 | 1,389 | 1,793 | 1,952 | 2,369 | 2,698 |
| | Per cent | 100 | 100 | 100 | 100 | 100 | 100 |
| Central government services | £ million | 707 | 1,201 | 1,537 | 1,685 | 1,968 | 2,217 |
| | Per cent | 88.0 | 86.5 | 85.7 | 86.3 | 83.1 | 82.2 |
| Consolidated Fund | £ million | 568 | 1,007 | 1,304 | 1,447 | 1,688 | 1,900 |
| | Per cent | 70.7 | 72.5 | 72.7 | 74.1 | 71.3 | 70.4 |
| Insurance Stamp contributions | £ million | 102 | 160 | 181 | 175 | 213 | 228 |
| | Per cent | 12.7 | 11.5 | 10.1 | 9.0 | 9.0 | 8.5 |
| Charges to recipients | £ million | 35 | 31 | 47 | 59 | 62 | 79 |
| | Per cent | 4.4 | 2.3 | 2.6 | 3.0 | 2.6 | 2.9 |
| Miscellaneous | £ million | 2 | 3 | 5 | 4 | 5 | 10 |
| | Per cent | 0.2 | 0.2 | 0.3 | 0.2 | 0.2 | 0.4 |
| Local authority services | £ million | 96 | 188 | 256 | 267 | 401 | 481 |
| | Per cent | 12.0 | 13.5 | 14.3 | 13.7 | 16.9 | 17.6 |
| Rates and Consolidated Fund grants | £ million | 83 | 161 | 223 | 233 | 356 | 429 |
| | Per cent | 10.4 | 11.6 | 12.4 | 11.9 | 15.0 | 15.9 |
| Charges to recipients | £ million | 13 | 27 | 33 | 34 | 45 | 52 |
| | Per cent | 1.6 | 1.9 | 1.9 | 1.8 | 1.9 | 1.9 |

*Source: Health and Personal Social Services Statistics, London, HMSO, 1973.*

more effective co-ordination between various parts of the NHS and to make it at once more controllable from the centre and more sensitive to local feeling. As Michael Cooper has said, however, the real hope for the new system 'is that it improves the *capacity* of the NHS for improvement' (Cooper, 1975). But it plainly does so less than perfectly. Save in Northern Ireland, the personal social services are not integrated into this structure and the local authority management units of the one do not always correspond to the other. Community health councils (CHCs) are based on the district and are intended to introduce the democratic element of the local public interest into the structure. The members of the CHCs are appointed — not elected — by local authorities, voluntary associations and the RHA. Moreover, they have no direct control over the management of the NHS and, although they have powers to obtain any information they require and to inspect institutions, they lack the evaluative services of experts of their own and a national organisation. Their authority is essentially limited to that of reporting back. Currently some (rather half-hearted) ways of strengthening CHCs and of providing them with a national council of CHCs are under discussion. Whether the management of the NHS will, under the new arrangements, turn out to be less authoritarian and medical-dominated, and more subject to local pressures for efficiency and humanity in non-clinical matters, and to central pressures for efficiency in all matters, remains to be seen. The *sine qua non* of efficient management remains, of course, the technology of monitoring and controlling the doctors, with which this book is principally concerned. As these become more developed, and provided that central authorities use the financial powers that ultimately they possess (but largely forbore from using in the first twenty-five years of the NHS), then the possibility of a co-ordinated, open and efficient service is plainly there. But, ultimately, this will require a brave facing up to the traditional authoritarianism of the medical profession which has so frequently in the past flouted the advice of central circulars (see, e.g., Haywood, 1974).

## II  WEST GERMANY

Whereas in Britain the modern welfare state system of health provision developed out of ideas traceable back to the nineteenth century Poor Law system, with the interwar period constituting only a brief flirtation with compulsory social insurance, in Germany a historically early (1883) emphasis was put on social insurance and this has continued to the present day, with the 'public assistance' approach (universalised in Britain) playing only a small and residual role.

Health care in modern Germany has grown directly from the Bismarckian legislation of 1883 and is highly decentralised. Today, 90.5 per cent of the population are covered by the compulsory insurance scheme, 8.6 per cent are privately insured and 0.9 per cent are without insurance but are entitled to receive, after a means test, 'Social Aid' from the provincial government according to need.

Social insurance provides free medical and dental care, and cost-sharing arrangements, as in Britain, exist for prescription drugs, dentures, etc. The system is regulated and supervised by the government and, while the local authorities under provincial governments provide specific services (such as public health measures, school health; responsibility for the care of the handicapped, addicts, the chronic sick etc. and supervision of the hospitals), the medical system is principally adminstered by 1,627 Sickness Funds. Wage-earners and those salaried employees and the self-employed with incomes below a limit are compulsorily insured (together with dependents) under one or other of the various types of fund, depending, for example, upon area of residence, workplace or occupation, while those earning above the limit have the option to join.

The Sickness Funds operate as autonomous bodies under the law but must report to the provincial governments which supervise their financial stability. All funds provide publicly prescribed basic benefits but differ in supplementary benefits for largely the same reasons as did the approved societies in interwar Britain. The main source of finance for health care in Germany is contributions from employees and a payroll 'tax' on employers (received by the insurance funds) with an equal yield per insured person save for the very poor, unemployed, pensioners, etc., who make no contribution. Additional contributions come to the Funds from the federal government (for maternity allowances) and from pension funds on behalf of pensioners. In addition, direct payments are made to hospitals, 1,330 of which are publicly owned. The rest are either charitable (1,217) or private (947).

As in Britain, out-of-pocket cash payments by German patients are restricted to dentures, etc. (and there are no charges for dental treatment not requiring appliances). The patient presents himself to a doctor on the panel of his Sickness Fund, and the doctor then has complete clinical freedom to decide treatment, and may send him to a local specialist, many of whom work outside the hospitals, or to a hospital. The doctors are paid on a fee per item of service basis by the Sickness Funds via the local Panel Doctors' Association on a scale agreed between the profession and the funds at federal level. There are also professional bodies (similar to the British General Medical Council) with the power to dicipline members.

Public and charitable hospitals are obliged to accept Sickness Fund patients and are paid by the Funds according to a federal daily flat amount for basic care which is less than daily cost, the balance being made up either by the charity operating the hospital or the government. Additional hotel facilities etc. are obtainable at a higher charge, for which many people take out additional (private) insurance. Hospital doctors are salaried, and, as in Britain, only consultants may take private patients.

Table 10.6 shows the income and expenditure of the Funds over the period 1938–73. During the 1960s current expenditure grew, according to these data, at a lower rate than in most West European countries (around 10 per cent per year) – an effect at least partially attributable to Germany's relatively successful record in containing inflation. But it should also be recalled that the data here include some elements (e.g. cash benefits) and exclude others (e.g. private expenditure and some government hospital finance) that make comparisons with Britain hazardous. Table 10.2 above, however, confirms that, at least in the 1960s, the rate of growth of real expenditure in Germany was relatively slower than in other advanced countries save Britain. The problem of recurring deficits in the Funds (and in the hospitals too, save mainly for the private profit-making hospitals located mainly in spa towns) and the necessity for governmental supplementation suggests that the question of control over the medical profession is as burning a matter – and likely to become increasingly so – in Germany as in Britain.

Organisational differences between the two countries lead in the predicted direction. For example, the average length of acute hospitals' in-patient stay in Germany in 1971 was 19.9 days compared with 10.4 days in Britain, which, while consistent with a relatively lower endowment of beds for the chronically sick and geriatrics (so that more such cases may overflow into acute beds than in the UK), is also consistent with a *per diem* basis of charge, which means that each additional patient day will add to overheads while, beyond a certain point, imposing only hotel costs. The number of admissions at 150 per

TABLE 10.6.

Social insurance income and expenditure, 1938–73 (million DM)

| Year (1) | Income (2) | Expenditure (3) | Deficit/ surplus (4) | Types of expenditure* | | | | |
|---|---|---|---|---|---|---|---|---|
| | | | | Medical and dental (5) | Medicines appliances (6) | Hospital treatment (7) | Cash sickness benefits (8) |
| 1938 | 1,803 | 1,787 | 16 | 526 (29) | 205 (11) | 205 (11) | 397 (22) |
| 1950 | 2,422 | 2,278 | 144 | 568 (24) | 438 (19) | 438 (19) | 469 (20) |
| 1955 | 4,617 | 4,627 | −10 | 1,276 (17) | 826 (17) | 709 (15) | 938 (20) |
| 1960 | 9,524 | 9,513 | 11 | 2,342 (24) | 1,568 (16) | 1,362 (14) | 2,572 (27) |
| 1965 | 15,961 | 15,785 | 176 | 4,148 (26) | 2,947 (18) | 2,422 (15) | 3,501 (22) |
| 1966 | 18,554 | 18,362 | 192 | 5,109 (27) | 2,940 (16) | 3,397 (18) | 3,791 (20) |
| 1967 | 19,738 | 19,236 | 502 | 5,400 (28) | 3,325 (17) | 3,851 (20) | 3,301 (17) |
| 1968 | 21,195 | 21,513 | −318 | 5,844 (27) | 4,390 (20) | 4,384 (20) | 3,967 (18) |
| 1969 | 23,315 | 23,734 | −419 | 6,284 (26) | 4,989 (21) | 5,042 (21) | 4,186 (17) |
| 1970 | 26,116 | 25,179 | 937 | 7,166 (28) | 5,052 (20) | 6,009 (24) | 2,304 (9) |
| 1971 | 31,279 | 31,140 | 139 | 8,831 (28) | 6,179 (20) | 7,653 (25) | 2,958 (9) |
| 1972 | 36,213 | 36,401 | −188 | 9,836 (27) | 8,426 (23) | 9,265 (25) | 3,450 (9) |
| 1973 | 43,652 | 42,750 | 902 | 10,799 (25) | 9,871 (23) | 11,307 (26) | 3,941 (9) |

*The expenditures do not add up to the years totals (or 100%) because only the most important categories are listed. Exemptions include cash maternity and death benefits, administrative costs.

Source: Maynard (1975) to 1969; Schewe et al. (1975) for 1970–73.

1,000 population was substantially higher than in the UK where it stood at 115, and this is probably largely the result of the relative paucity of out-patient facilities compared with Britain, itself in turn plausibly attributable to the fee-per-item basis of remuneration for community physicians which encourages specialisation at a very local level and a reluctance to refer unless the medical indications are strong and clear.

In each country, physicians may prescribe the drugs they think appropriate subject to relatively light controls on over-prescribing, and the patient pays only a nominal price. The drug bill is effectively the product of physician judgement and the prices set by the pharmaceutical industry. In Germany about 28 per cent of medical expenditure is on drugs compared with about 10 per cent in the NHS. Most of this differential must be attributed to the success of the British government in controlling pharmaceutical prices, which have been estimated (see Cooper and Cooper, 1972) to be between 27 and 35 per cent higher in Germany than Britain. Moreover, in Britain there is the serious prospect that the freedom of GPs' prescription will be restricted in the forseeable future to those preparations on an 'approved' list.

## III  CANADA

The Canadian system of health insurance is still in a process of evolution. Constitutionally, the provinces have jurisdiction over health care matters (save for public health, which is a federal concern), and each has evolved its own particular arrangements which, however, have certain common features owing to the fact of federal subsidies. These features are: universal access to health care, transferability of rights from province to province, comprehensive coverage (which effectively means compulsory insurance) and non-profit administration. Six of the provinces require no premiums or contributions. In others there are small contributions from the insured and in Ontario there is a small (0.8 per cent) payroll tax on employers for health care. Contributions are reduced or eliminated for the poor in these provinces.

The principal sources of finance, however, as in Britain (but unlike Germany), are governmental. The federal government contributes about half the cost of the hospital and primary care systems in the provinces and this is financed from a 2 per cent federal income tax surcharge up to a $100 limit. At the provincial level, health care is financed out of general revenues save for the premiums charged in some provinces. In one or two others special taxes are earmarked for health care (e.g. the property tax in Alberta or the sales tax in British Columbia and Nova Scotia). In some provinces small charges are also imposed at the point of use (but drugs are fully paid for by the patient — save in hospitals and for the elderly or unemployed in some provinces).

Physicians are paid, as in Germany, on a fee-per-service basis according to fee schedules drawn up on a provincial basis by the provincial medical association and the provincial government. In most provinces, however, the doctor receives only a portion of the fee from the State and the doctor may bill the patient (provided the patient has been notified beforehand) for the difference (usually 10 or 15 per cent of the scheduled fee). Doctors may however opt out of the medical care plan and bill patients directly. Again, patients must be informed beforehand. In this latter case, fees are often set at a rate above the schedule — a practice termed 'extra-billing', so that patients, who under this arrangement submit their bills for repayment to the provincial government, pay a balance themselves, being reimbursed only the scheduled amount. (In Quebec no reimbursement is allowed for patients using doctors who have opted out.)

The hospitals provide free services, but patients may choose semi-private or private accommodation, in which case fees are charged. In some provinces the hospitals are not permitted to keep any — or are allowed to keep only a portion — of this additional income.

The notion of 'comprehensiveness' of care is a good deal more restricted in Canada than in the NHS or in Germany. In addition to the drugs and better hotel facilities referred to above, for which the patient must pay, he also pays for dental care, ambulance services, hearing aids, spectacles, etc. Mainly for this reason, private insurance continues in Canada at a larger level than in Britain or Germany. All medical expenses are, however, tax deductible and private insurance agents are prevented by law from duplicating the public arrangements (thus, one cannot insure for physician's care under the public arrangements).

We noted, when looking at the German arrangements, that fee-for-service gives a financial incentive for doctors to increase the number of (billable!) services to the consumer and to discourage the patient from using substitute services (e.g., self-care; prevention). There is ample empirical evidence from Canada that these incentives work — for example, when the schedules are revised, those items whose *relative* price rises are increasingly supplied to patients (*Task Force Report*, 1970).

Also like Germany, the independence of the medical practitioners from the ultimate sources of finance makes them exceedingly difficult to control (even in the NHS control is difficult, but the controls are at least direct and bilateral). In fee-for-service systems, physician incomes can easily be maintained or increased by the physicians increasing their patients' demand for health care and there is ample evidence that this is what they do (Evans, 1974).

Peculiar to Canada is the federal—provincial cost-sharing arrangement. Effectively, this implies that every dollar's worth of expenditure (on federally 'shareable' items) costs the province only 50c. Not only is this a direct incentive for increased spending, but it also tends to focus spending on 'shareable' items. Although full participation by all provinces in the medical care plan was not achieved until 1971, it is scarcely surprising, in view of all these factors, that table 10.2 shows Canada increasing the share of GNP devoted to health care faster than other countries. Table 10.7, taken in conjunction with table 10.2, shows that this growth rate has accelerated alongside the development of the programme and also provides some details.

It is perhaps worth pointing out that the transition in Canada from a private insurance system to compulsory public insurance does not

TABLE 10.7.
*Growth of Canadian health care expenditure (annual rates)*

|  | 1953—71 | 1960—71 |
|---|---|---|
|  | % | % |
| General and allied special hospitals | 13.2 | 14.1 |
| Other hospitals | 8.7 | 9.5 |
| Nursing homes | — | 14.8 |
| Physicians | 11.4 | 13.0 |
| Dentists | 9.3 | 10.0 |
| Other health professionals | — | 7.5 |
| Prescription drugs | 10.6* | 11.1 |
| Over-the-counter drugs | — | 9.5 |
| Eyeglasses and appliances | — | 8.0 |
| Administration, research, construction, etc. | — | 7.5 |
| Total (above items) | 12.0* | 11.8 |

*1957—71
*Source*: Evans (1975b)

appear to have caused any marked increases in utilisation chiefly because, as we have seen in chapter 7, under private insurance the patient who is insured faced low or zero charges at the point of use.

## IV CONCLUSIONS

In each of our three countries the great achievement has been to remove financial anxiety from sickness. The manner in which this has been done however varies dramatically, with the State having substantial potential powers to control costs in Britain, more limited powers in Germany and very few at all in Canada. The same ranking holds with respect to the ability of the government to ensure effective and efficient operation of the health services. In each country however the indications are that citizens are mighty pleased with 'free' care – and this built-in popular reaction against reform, together with professional vested interests, makes the enormous problems anticipated, experienced and struggled with by academics and administrators extremely difficult to solve in a satisfactory way. The same forces, as we have seen before, have also held back the development of conceptual and practical tools for management. But it is hard to resist the temptation of inferring that these problems are going to be a great deal easier to solve in Britain than in most other countries.

## BIBLIOGRAPHY

Abel-Smith, B. (1967) *An International Study of Health Expenditure* Geneva, WHO

Andreopoulos, S. (ed.) (1975) *National Health Insurance: Can We Learn from Canada?* New York, Wiley

Cooper, M. H. (1975) *Rationing Health Care* London, Croom Helm

Cooper, M. H. and Cooper, A. J. (1972) *International Price Comparisons* London, HMSO for NEDC

Cooper, M. H. and Culyer, A. J. (1970) 'An economic assessment of some aspects of the organisation of the NHS' in Jones (1970)

Department of National Health and Welfare (1974) *Social Security in Canada* Ottawa, Queen's Printer

Evans, R. G. (1974) 'Supplier-induced demand – some empirical evidence and implications' in Perlman (1974)

Evans R. G. (1975a) 'Beyond the medical market place: expenditure, utilization, and pricing of insured health care in Canada' in Rosett (1975)

Evans, R. G. (1975b) 'Health Costs and Expenditures in Canada' (forthcoming in proceedings of an International Conference on Health Costs and Expenditures at the Fogarty International Center, Washington DC)

Haywood, S. C. (1974) *Managing the Health Service* London, Allen and Unwin

Jones, I. M. (ed.) (1970) *Health Services Financing* London, British Medical Association

Kastner, F. (1968) *Monograph on the Organisation of Medical Care within the Framework of Social Security* Geneva, ILO

Lees, D. S. and Cooper, M. H. (1964) 'Fee per item of service – Manchester and Salford 1913–28' *Medical Care*, vol. 2

Lees, D. S. *et al.* (1964) *Monopoly or choice in Health Services* London, Institute of Economic affairs

Lichtner, S. and Pflanz, M. (1971) 'Appendectomy in the Federal Republic of Germany: epidemiology and medical care reform' *Medical Care*, vol. 9

Maynard, A. K. (1975) *Health Care in the European Community* London, Croom Helm

Maxwell, R. (1974) *Health Care : the Growing Dilemma* New York, McKinsey

Office of Health Economics (1970) 'International health expenditure' *OHE Information Sheet* No. 9, London, OHE

Office of Health Economics (1973) 'International health expenditures' *OHE Information Sheet No. 22* London, OHE

Perlman, M. (ed.) (1974) *The Economics of Health and Medical Care* London, Macmillan

Political and Economic Planning (1937) *Report on the British Health Services* London, PEP

Rosett, R. (ed.) (1975) *The Role of Health Insurance in the Health Services Sector* New York, Columbia University Press

Ruderman, A. P. (1970) 'The organisation and financing of medical care in Canada' in Jones (1970)

Schewe, D. *et al.* (1975) *Übersicht über die Soziale Sicherung*, Herausgeber: der Bundesminister für Arbeit und Sozialordnung, Bonn

Schreiber, W. (1970) 'Health insurance in the German Federal Republic' in Jones (1970)

Simanis, J. G. (1973) 'Medical care expenditures in seven countries' *Social Security Bulletin*, vol. 36

Simanis, J. G. (1975) *National Health Systems in Eight Countries* Washington DC, Department of Health, Education and Welfare

*Task Force Report on Costs of Health Services in Canada* (1970) Ottawa, Queen's Printer

Titmuss, R. M. (1968) *Commitment to Welfare*, London, Allen and Unwin.

Weisbrod, B. (1964) 'Collective-consumption services of individual-consumption goods' *Quarterly Journal of Economics*, vol. 78

# 11. The NHS — an Assessment

This book has been about need and how best to meet it. It is, perhaps, unfortunate that we should be lumbered with such a term, which both has prominent persuasive overtones and lends itself to vague and various interpretations. Our own interpretation has been to emphasise that need is not, nor ever was, purely a technical matter, and that it does indeed require the exercise of moral judgements in defining what the needs are and which of them are, at the margin, more important than others. The crucial question at the heart of the politics of the NHS is who should be making these judgements? Certainly not the author, or social scientists in general, or the medics; for while there does exist a school of thought that argues that, because 'experts' ' opinions about the facts, the history, the technology etc. involve both expertise *and* judgement, their moral judgements also have some special authority. Nothing could be more dangerous than this view to democracy in general in a technical age of large organisations, and nothing could be more alien to the idea of the NHS. Admittedly, however, such a view is – predictably – popular among the professionals (and not only in medicine) and their trade unions, whose deplorable arrogance is a feature of our producer-oriented times.

In the NHS, the experts can help first of all in making clear the differences in the kinds of judgements that have to be made, and in devising concepts and presenting information that helps them to be made in a more effective and aware way. If, then, in this book we have focused a great deal on this kind of interpretation of 'need', that is because such a focus has been long overdue. We have muddled through for long enough.

Our unashamedly economic approach has also had the great virtue of encouraging a broader concentration on the social aspects of decision-making in the NHS, rather than on the financial aspects, while at the same time retaining the ends—means approach that is essential for proper management and proper policy formation. Only the end can justify the means. The end of the NHS is not the NHS. In Britain the end — effective, efficient and fair health care — is to be served by the means of the NHS. It is of course possible that this means is contrary to or inconsistent with the end. But we have tried to present a large number of reasons why this is not the case, all of which can be ultimately classified under two broad heads: the public nature (via spill-overs and the like) of the objectives on the one hand and the appropriateness of alternative institutional forms in achieving the objectives on the other.

Much of the argument about the NHS in the 1950s and 1960s focused on the latter. In our judgement, this mostly *a priori* argument about what is essentially an *empirical* question was largely misplaced. The evidence, we believe, suggests that health care is an area where public ownership and a substantial diminution of the role of consumer prices is more effective a way of organisation than others (see chapter 7). But the reasons for this lie less on the demand side (as the NHS defenders of the 1960s argued) and more — much more — on the supply side. The NHS has, of course, failed notably to realise many of the potential benefits of 'rationalising' supply, and the revolution — or evolution — to come will be concentrated here. At the same time, however, it must be acknowledged that a residuum of the political issues underlying the NHS debate of the 1960s remains an inherent danger in the NHS structure, for central to either a Marxist or a liberal philosophy is the view that the State is an instrument of oppression; that for Marxists it serves to entrench the position of the ruling class and that, for liberals, it does both this and removes power, discretion and freedom of action and choice from the individual citizen. In health care, with its traditions of authority and hierarchy within its professions and in its relations with the public, these dangers are real and have recently been confirmed dramatically in the NHS especially with regard to long-stay patients (Robb, 1967; official reports on hospitals at Ely, 1969; Farleigh, 1971; Whittingham, 1972; Ockendon 1974). Nursing, where contact with the patient is often most intimate, is famous for its harridans. Haywood (1974) reports a typical story: ' "We did away with restrictions ages ago," said one matron, weightily propelling me past a large notice: Visiting from 4.30 to 5.0 p.m. daily. Identical placards hung outside all the wards. "We keep them up," Matron smiled at my naive mystification "because otherwise visitors [to a children's ward] would think they could pop in any time." '

These dangers are also, of course, present in more decentralised and competitive systems but are probably more real in a state-owned system that is heavily dominated by the medical professions. Against them the patient, either individually or collectively in a market situation, has little effective countervailing power, for though profit is clearly the driving force of many medical practitioners, their incomes and the patient's satisfaction with the competence and considerateness of care are tenuously related. The NHS organisation does, however, have the potential to control the professionals and to monitor their performance in the light of socially, not merely medically, determined objectives. It is this element that at once both 'justifies' the NHS and which has, sadly, been largely lacking in its performance to date.

In the anti-medicine brigade, Ivan Illich (1975) must be the arch *advocatus diaboli*, for in his view the medics (as well as the industrial state) are destroying man's very humanity:

The true miracle of modern medicine is diabolical. It consists not only of making individuals but whole populations survive on inhumanly low levels of personal health. That health should decline with increasing health service delivery is unforeseen only by the health managers, precisely because their strategies are the result of their blindness to the inalienability of life . . . . Medical nemesis . . . is the expropriation of man's coping ability by a maintenance service which keeps him geared up at the service of the industrial system.

The arcadian remedies implicit in Illich's diagnosis of 'structural iatrogenesis' (iatrogenetic disease is that induced by medical practice) are neither generally desired in modern societies nor would they seem particularly desirable. But the remedies that our economic analysis implies are pretty far-reaching, and amount to a substantial erosion of what is often called 'clinical freedom'. Our analysis suggests : that the definition of health, or ill health, is not mainly a matter for doctors; that the establishment of social trade-offs is not mainly a matter for doctors; that judgement about the proper size of the NHS relative to other public and private spending categories is not mainly a matter for doctors; that judgement about which cares and cures are to be available under the NHS is not mainly a matter for doctors; that judgement about the resource inputs, including manpower, required to provide these cares and cures is only partially a matter for doctors; that the monitoring of medical inefficiency, incompetence and carelessness ought to be much more the concern of doctors (and others too); and that evaluation of the clinical and social effectiveness of clinical procedures should be very much more the preoccupation of doctors (Culyer, 1975).

Much of the book has, of course, been devoted to the problems that arise in trying to formulate methods by which better decisions about all of these things may be made. In total, they do not warrant the conclusion that Britain's health has been badly served by the NHS compared with other countries, nor that we spend too little on health care. But neither do they warrant the reverse conclusion. What, in total, they do warrant is a massive research programme into the effectiveness of unvalidated clinical procedures and further development and application of the efficiency evaluation techniques we have sought to indicate in this book, with special attention being given to objectives: the meeting of needs.

The politically most challenging aspect of all lies not so much in the inculcation of notions of effective use of means for defined ends at the *management* level — though there are battles here to be fought and won — as in ensuring that efficient management decisions are carried out at the level of clinical practice. In the very short term, effective monitoring of results at this level (or indeed most others too) is difficult because of the absence of routine status measurement data of the sort described in chapters 4 and 8. But in the fullness of time we can envisage monitoring at, say, the GP level that might take the following form: a periodic sample is taken of the ten or so most frequent conditions constituting the bulk of the GPs' routine work and of how the outcomes for patients treated differed at some appropriate statistical level of significance from those of norms established by, say, studies of 'best practice'. A marked adverse deviation would warrant the GP being called to explain this. There may, of course, be perfectly legitimate explanations (e.g. poor support facilities), which themselves would then become the object for further examination. There may also, however, be incompetence in the sense that the individual himself is operating in a way inconsistent with the objective of the NHS in maximising, out of given resources, the reduction in need. As Michael Cooper has pointedly observed: 'the aircrews of passenger air services are given Ministry approved checks every thirteen months. Cabin crews are given yearly survival and emergency checks. Are surgeons really any less susceptible to obsolescence, sickness or incompetence?' (Cooper, 1975).

Even in the shorter term, however, some progress in the spirit of effectiveness monitoring could be made. Today it would be fairly easy to compare crude outcome variations as between different GPs and different hospitals (and hospital doctors) in terms of death rates, hospital fatality rates, re-admission rates, speed of return to work. Practitioners and institutions with marked deviations from a middle range could (after relevant associated data concerning population age and sex structures, hospital case mix, etc.) be called upon to explain. Often, advice and information about the procedures adopted by others might be sufficient a corrective in those cases where no satisfactory explanation for the divergence can be offered. But in some cases more ultimate sanctions of a financial sort or, in the limit, of even being struck off the medical register for incompetence may have to be used.

In the longer term, much finer measures of effectiveness and cost effectiveness will be developed, related not only to the treatments actually given but also to the impact of medical care in each area's needs. At this stage the processes of planning, monitoring and controlling will have become highly complementary.

For some (perhaps the professionals), the vision will appear to be an authoritarian nightmare – despite the fact that most researchers (for example) manage to cope quite capably with the period reviews and inspections that government research councils make of programmes they sponsor. To others (who focus more on the clients of the system) the NHS appears already to be a highly authoritarian institution.

The charge has frequently been made against the NHS (especially by the libertarians and others who are not easily fobbed off with assurances about the social responsibility of managers, professionals and scientists in large organisations, both public and private) that it is a quintessentially paternalist organisation. Indeed, we have already discussed the Titmussian arguments for denying any kind of rationality to individuals as patients. More generally, it is a measure of the generation gap that, in an age when the young intelligentsia is becoming increasingly libertarian and 'small-is-beautiful' in its social outlook, their elders having positions of power in society persist in unimaginative attempts to assuage these reasonable sceptics by assurances about their social intentions – despite the absence of social accountability. Thus the high priests of capitalism seek to correct its 'unacceptable' face by averring that the job of businessmen is to serve the interests of society (usually and conveniently left undefined), whereas their job is quite plainly to serve the interests of their shareholder/owners (subject to whatever social controls *Parliament* imposes on their activity). It is also quite plain that in pursuing profit and so serving these interests they may also serve (thought this is merely instrumental) the wider community.

If there are lamentably few these days, however, to argue that profit-seeking may sometimes serve a useful social function, so there are even fewer around to explain what it is, especially in the public sector, that is to replace 'profit' as the general objective and as the general indicator of 'success'. There are, indeed, good reasons to view the paternalists with disquiet, for whenever they appear on the scene, clarity of objective, efficiency of means of achieving it and account-ability to those on whose behalf it is supposed to be being achieved all tend to fly out of the window.

Yet there is a quite specific case for a paternalism of sorts in the NHS. It is not a negative case built upon the alleged irrationalities of individuals as patients (which is hardly an argument *for* anything at all!), but a positive case built upon the simple observation of what seems a quite indisputable fact: that in many (but not necessarily all) matters of health care, individuals wish to delegate decisions to others to act on their behalf. From this flows the argument for public ownership (as opposed merely to subsidy) as we saw in chapter 7, the definition of the NHS objective as reducing need efficiently, the definition of need and the meaning of efficiency. From it also flows the desirability of monitoring and controlling those to whom these important decisions have been delegated.

It is arguable, of course, that the framework we have developed here is not at all paternalist — at least in the traditional 'merit good' sense common in economics, or in the sense of beneficent coercion in political theory. In practice these traditional uses of the term invariably turn out to be merely fancy names for a more or less muddled, and more or less inefficient authoritarianism. By contrast, our vision is of an NHS serving individuals' unambiguous needs, with an unambiguous procedure for evaluating such needs and establishing priorities, and with an unambiguous procedure for ensuring that the producers in the system are the properly monitored and controlled servants of their clients.

While the word 'need' has been prominent in the rhetoric of the

NHS, its effective utilisation as a concept to produce the results the NHS aspires to has been notably absent. In this book we have tried to reformulate the old questions in such a way that they suggest practical means by which these aspirations may be realised. Much work remains to be done, of course, but done it must be, as must the objections of the vested interests be resisted and refuted, if the NHS is truly to live up to any testable claim that it is the 'best in the world'. The job cannot be one for the faint-hearted, and if this book can help rationally to persuade the unconvinced of its necessity as well as rallying the faithful to stand by the ideals of the NHS as they really are – and as they can be implemented – then its writing will have been more than worthwhile.

## BIBLIOGRAPHY

Cooper, M. H. (1975) *Rationing Health Care* London, Croom Helm; New York, Halstead

Culyer, A. J. (1975) 'Health : the social cost of doctors' discretion' *New Society*, 27 February

Ely Report (1969) *Report of Committee of Enquiry into Allegations of Ill-treatment of Patients and Other Irregularities at the Ely Hospital Cardiff* Cmnd. 3975, London, HMSO

Farleigh Report (1971) *Report of the Farleigh Hospital Committee of Inquiry* Cmnd. 4557, London, HMSO

Haywood, S. C. (1974) *Managing the Health Service* London, Allen and Unwin

Illich, I. (1975) *Medical Nemesis : The Expropriation of Health* London, Calder and Boyars

Ockendon Report (1974) *Report of the Committee of Inquiry into South Ockendon Hospital* H.C.124, London, HMSO

Robb, B. (1967) *Sans Everything : A Case to Answer* London, Association for the Elderly in Government Institutions

Whittingham Report (1972) *Report of the Committee of Inquiry into the Whittingham Hospital* Cmnd 4861, London, HMSO

# Questions for Discussion

1. *Abolishing need.* It is sometimes argued that all health needs should be eliminated. Is there any definition of 'need' that would enable this to be possible? Is there any definition of 'need' that would make it desirable?

2. *Priorities.* On page 105 there is a list of five factors that are suggested as being likely to figure in anyone's list of considerations for inclusion in an admissions priority index. Yet at no time are these factors ranked in order of priority one after the other. Indeed, it would have been quite against the logic of chapter 7 — and indeed the whole book — so to have ranked them. Why? How is it suggested that priorities ought to be established? (The answer has nothing to do with questions concerning *who* should establish priorities.)

3. *Market versus State.* Why is it not possible to infer that the NHS is preferable to an insurance-based system and markets for health care on the basis of arguments about the nature of the *demand* for care (e.g. consumer ignorance or high cost of care), while it is possible to base a case for the NHS against the market on the basis of supply considerations?

4. *Private practice.* Private insurance for hospital health care outside the NHS can be purchased by the average family man for about the same monthly premium as the rental on a colour television set. Private treatment brings several advantages: choice of hospital doctor (if you

have a preference); privacy for those who prefer to be ill in private (but may not 'need' single or small room in hospital on clinical grounds); greater choice about when you are admitted; and usually better 'hotel' facilities (telephone, television, menus, etc.) Yet despite this, trade unions do not offer this as a benefit of membership (they could, by arrangement with the insurance companies, arrange reductions in premiums by forming a group plan), nor do they seek this as a fringe benefit to be got from employers. Why do you think this is the case? Could it be that they simply do not value the extra benefits enough? (If so, why do they often seek to prevent others from having them?) Or do you think that they object to it on the moral ground that private practice creates unequal opportunities? (Yet the premiums are quite modest relative to other things that ordinary working people spend their money on.) Or do you think that they believe that private care is more costly to insure for than it actually is? (In which case why have the insurance agencies not disabused them?) Or is there some other explanation?

5. *Monitoring doctors.*    What arguments would you adduce *for* the view that only doctors know what is good for patients and that their actions should be monitored only by other doctors? (If you cannot think of any such arguments, adduce those for the contrary view: that the role of doctors should be quite specific and, even in clinical situations, should be subject to substantial control.)

6. *The value of life.*    How much would you pay now to reduce the probability of your dying from a disease or an accident in the next ten years by one per cent? (Be honest, now.) How much would you like me to pay to reduce the probability of *your* dying in the next ten years by one per cent? (Again, be honest!) How much would you pay to reduce the probability of *my* dying (me, a stranger) in the next ten years by one per cent?

7. *Bribing doctors.*    Suppose the doctors would accept a reformed NHS in which their professional judgements and actions were far more stringently monitored and controlled than at present only if their salaries were doubled. Should we double their salaries?

8. *Controlling emigration.*    Suppose doctors started emigrating on an unprecedented scale. Should one raise their salaries (or improve conditions of service), or should one ban emigration on the grounds

that they are depriving the community of the return on the investment the community has put into them or compel them to bear more of the cost of the investment in the first place? When, if ever, would it be moral to proscribe emigration? Consider your answer with respect to: school teachers; university professors; nurses; other workers (social workers, retrained workers, for example) who have been through government-subsidised training schemes; anyone who has had higher education; anyone who has had compulsory education.

9. *Doctor immigration.* The NHS imports many doctors from overseas. Ostensibly these doctors came in the first instance for additional training, but it is training that is largely unnecessary in the poorer countries from which most of them come: in the Indian subcontinent there is no shortage of hospital doctors but a chronic shortage of doctors in rural areas with relatively simple skills. Who gains from this process and who loses? Should rural doctors in the Indian subcontinent be paid more than hospital doctors there in the major centres? Is the NHS exploiting the poor countries? Is the NHS exploiting overseas doctors? Are the relevant overseas countries exploiting their rural populations? Are the overseas hospital doctors exploiting their rural as well their urban populations? In what sense(s) do you understand the term 'exploit'?

10. *Ineffective health care.* Should people be entitled to receive ineffective care if they demand it? In the NHS? In the private sector?

11. *Need.* Need is a kind of demand. But whose demand? Whose demand *should* it be in the NHS?

12. *Hospital objectives.* Suppose (making a big imaginative effort) that British hospitals were profit-making organisations. They would then seek to maximise their profit. *What do you think they seek to maximise under the NHS? What evidence would you seek to *refute* your hypothesised answer? Does whatever evidence you can lay hands on refute it? If it does (it probably does), return to the asterisk.

13. *Health needs and personal income.* In the text, it was argued that income or wealth should be an *irrelevance* in meeting health care needs. Why? If you disagree with the argument, what relevance do you think income or wealth does have in saying what the allocation ought to be?

14. *Regional allocation.*    Why is the present distribution of NHS resources what it is? Is it fair? If so why? If not, why not? Is your notion of fairness related to inputs (beds, doctors, etc.) or to the meeting of need? If you do not know whether it is fair or not, and your reason is not that you have no concept of 'fairness' but that you have insufficient relevant evidence, how do you account for this state of affairs after nearly thirty years of a service founded on the principles of fairness?

15. *Shortages.*    Of what is there the greatest shortage currently in the NHS: doctors, nurses, hospitals, renal dialysis machines, medical social workers, research into effective treatments, research into 'need', research into outcome measurement? Justify your putting some of these *below* others in your order or priority. What is a shortage?

16. *Demand for health.*    Why do some people of the same age expect with good reason to die sooner than others? Is that fair or unfair?

17. *Scarce skills.*    Some doctors are better at curing and caring for patients than others. Put more bluntly, some doctors kill or maim their patients more effectively than others. Such is inevitable, just as some economists, architects, solicitors, bricklayers, are worse than others. What do you think are the arguments for and against patients knowing the 'success' and 'failure' rates of their doctors? (Can 'success' and 'failure' be measured?)

18. *Cost—benefit analysis and 'benefit'.*    Chapter 5 criticised several of the characteristic treatments by economists and others of the 'benefit' side of cost—benefit analysis in health care. How do you think the benefits should, in general, be reckoned?

19. *Cost—benefit analysis and 'cost'.*    What is 'cost' in the sense used in this book? What are the advantages of this definition compared with other common definitions? Are there any disadvantages?

20. *Health indicators.*    For what purposes may it be useful to construct health status indicators? What form might the indicators take for each purpose? What information is given by an outcome or output indicator that cannot be given by provision or throughput indicators?

21. Who should die?

# Author Index

# Subject Index